The Attack On
PEARL HARBOR

D1522747

By Two Who Were There

Frank and Kay Tremaine

Cover painting by Robert McCall

Contents

Acknowledgments

To our friends, Rear Admiral Samuel R. Brown, Jr., (USN Ret.) and his wife, Anne; Captain James S. Gray (USN Ret.), Harry Albright and Peter S. Willett, we extend our thanks. They dredged their memories, dug out old diaries and records and generally refreshed our memories and supplied us with details we had forgotten or never known. Special thanks also to Jim Gray for finding and copying for us the War Diary of Fighting Six of the USS *Enterprise*.

We have drawn on Gordon W. Prange's monumental work, *At Dawn We Slept*, for certain specific information to support or supplement our own, particularly his research into the activity of the Japanese spy, Tadeo Yoshikawa.

In addition to the personal story he supplied, we also are indebted to Harry Albright for certain information drawn from his book, *Pearl Harbor, Japan's Fatal Blunder* in which he explores what might have happened had the Japanese followed the Pearl Harbor attack with an attempt to invade Hawaii.

For the description of the arrest of alien Japanese in Honolulu following the attack and their detention on Sand Island, we drew on the book *Hawaii, End of the Rainbow* by Dr. Kazuo Miyamoto.

Prologue

December 7, 1941.

Shortly before 8 a.m. on that peaceful Hawaiian Sunday morning, seven U.S. battleships rested at their berths along Battleship Row in Pearl Harbor. An eighth was in drydock across the channel. This was the battle line, the backbone of the U.S. Fleet.

Suddenly Japanese warplanes struck from east and west. The battleships erupted in flames and smoke.

Within minutes more than 1,000 men died on the battleship *Arizona* alone. Explosions blew off its bow and wracked its frame; fire roared through the ship throwing up a huge column of black smoke; it listed and settled on the shallow bottom, its forward mast tipping drunkenly.

The *Oklahoma* capsized and the other six dreadnaughts were disabled, three of them resting on the shallow bottom. Sheets of flaming oil floated on the water's surface hampering efforts to rescue men blown off the ships.

Men were blown apart, catapulted into the water or lay wounded on the decks. Their shipmates sprang into action.

Within minutes, guns on the stricken ships and ashore responded with a crescendo of fire. Japanese bombers and torpedo planes pressed their attack.

The biggest story of my career—of any newsman's career—had just dropped into my lap. I was asleep.

There were 86 American naval vessels in Pearl Harbor that morning. On many of them, chaplains were preparing for church services for the men and officers aboard. Many crewmen were ashore on leave.

There was a similar calm at other navy and army bases on the island of Oahu and in its only city, Honolulu

In Washington the Japanese ambassador and Japan's special envoy had requested a meeting with Secretary of State Cordell Hull at 1 p.m. (7:30 a.m. Hawaiian time). They were to deliver Japan's reply to the United States' recent hard-nosed statement of its position in the worsening Pacific crisis — only 25 minutes before the attack started.

As Hawaii awakened for another lazy Sunday, the first wave of Japanese carrier-borne warplanes approached from the northwest. At 7:48 a.m., divebombers screamed down on Kaneohe Naval Air Station across Oahu from Pearl Harbor.

At 7:55 a.m., the rest of the first wave struck. One group of bombers and torpedo planes concentrated on Battleship Row and the adjacent Ford Island Naval Air Station in Pearl Harbor. Other fighters and bombers knocked out the Army Air Corps' Hickam and Wheeler Fields and attacked Schofield Barracks, the big infantry base. The attack of the first wave lasted about half an hour. There was a lull of about 30 minutes, then a second wave roared in to finish the job.

When the last of the 350 warplanes turned northwestward to return to their six aircraft carriers and escorting ships nearly 200 miles away, the Japanese had knocked out Hawaii's air defenses and broken the back of the U.S. Pacific Fleet—or so they thought.

In addition to the battleships, the Japanese in less than two hours also had disabled or sunk three cruisers, five destroyers, a large floating drydock and four other vessels.

Their attacks on Oahu's airfields were so unexpected and so effective that probably fewer than 50 of the 475 flyable army and navy aircraft on the island got off the ground.

A year later, the navy said 3,303 American soldiers, sailors and Marines were killed or missing in the attack.

With only token aerial opposition, the attackers bored through the American ground fire to their targets. Estimates of their plane losses ranged from 29, according to the Japanese, to 105, according to the navy. A Japanese submarine plus five midget subs were lost, three of them inside Pearl Harbor

Pearl Harbor galvanized the American people and propelled them into World War II. It was an event whose effect on history still is being felt 50 years later. By bringing the United States into World War II, it turned near-defeat for the Allies into victory. That produced a peace which turned into a cold war between former allies and, at the same time, an economic resurgence of the vanquished unparalleled in history. In the postwar peace, Japan achieved more than it ever dreamed of winning in war and West Germany became more prosperous than ever before.

For many, Pearl Harbor also was very personal. For years it was said that Americans might forget birthdays, anniversaries or the names of their children but they could always tell you where they were and what they were doing on December 7, 1941 when they heard the news from Pearl Harbor.

For those who were there, it was more memorable. Each has his own story to tell. We are among them.

1 : The Navy Has "No Superior"

Honolulu was an interesting mixture in 1941—part major military base, part construction boom town, part bustling business center, part tourist haven. It was bursting its seams, but sugar cane and pineapple fields in the surrounding countryside still supported a touch of old Hawaiian plantation life.

All this coexisted in the midst of the lovely colors of sub-tropical flowers under an ever-present sun, cooled by the languid northeast trade winds.   Honolulu clung tenaciously to its title of *Paradise of the Pacific.*

We often had air raid drills and we were exhorted to dig bomb shelters in our lawns and gardens. News of the war in Europe and of the Pacific crisis caused by Japan's militaristic expansion in the Far East filled the papers. The army and navy held frequent practice alerts and we sometimes heard rumors of contact with Japanese submarines in Hawaiian waters. "Probably a sonar picked up a whale," a navy staff officer told me one day when I asked about such a report.

But despite the gathering clouds of war, Honolulu was a happy town, a town that enjoyed a party.

Except for the military, not many seemed to worry about war coming to Hawaii itself. Most people—civilians at least—considered the U.S. Pacific Fleet a protection, not a target. That the navy was pretty pleased with itself—at least the brass in Washington—might be seen in Secretary of Navy Frank Knox' annual report released for publication in Sunday's papers, December 7. He said that as a result of recent expansion, the U.S. Navy "has no superior in the world."

"I am proud to report," he said, "that the American people may feel fully confident in this navy. . . .On any comparable basis, the U.S. Navy is second to none."

Only a few months earlier, the Army Chief of Staff, General George C. Marshall, had told President Roosevelt, "The island of Oahu, due to its fortification, its garrison, and its physical characteristics, is believed to be the strongest fortress in the world."

Saturday, December 6, was like most other Saturdays in Honolulu. Tourists sunned on Waikiki Beach during the day, dined and danced that night on the beachside floor at the Royal Hawaiian hotel, under the huge banyan tree next door at the Moana hotel, or at Lau Yee Chai's, the big Chinese restaurant a couple of blocks from the beach.

Some Honoluluans joined the tourists but more entertained, or were entertained, in homes along the beaches, on the hills or snuggled in the valleys *mauka* (mau-kah—"toward the mountains") of the city.

If you were lucky and had friends in the Hawaiian community, you might have been invited to a backyard *luau* (loo-ow) to celebrate someone's birthday, anniversary or engagement. Then you'd have shown up in the afternoon in your colorful aloha shirt while the pig roasted in a stone-filled pit covered with *ti* (tee) leaves and dirt.

The Navy Has "No Superior"

You'd have drunk some beer or spirits, maybe even a little *okolehau* (oh-ko-lee-how), the strong Hawaiian liquor made from the ti root. If it was very good, it probably had aged in a cask slung beneath Grandma's rocking chair. You'd have listened to lovely voices singing old Hawaiian songs to strumming ukuleles and watched ladies of all sizes and shapes, and even some men, dancing the graceful authentic hula.

In the military, both officers and enlisted men had their clubs on the army and navy bases and they often had Saturday night dances. Single men, both civilian defense workers and restless young sailors and soldiers, roamed the bars and sometimes the brothels along River Street in Downtown Honolulu.

Military and civilians joined at some parties, both on the bases and in civilian homes. Most were pretty sedate affairs for, although there were lots of parties in Honolulu, it was pretty much a go-to-bed-early kind of town. Most parties seemed to end around midnight and that was the usual closing time for most public dine-and-dance places and for dances at the clubs. Of course, some of the less sedate folk thought that was party-pooping; their parties ran much later.

Admiral Husband E. Kimmel, Commander-in-Chief, U.S. Fleet, attended a small dinner party of about a dozen close friends given by Rear Admiral H. Fairfax Leary and his wife at the lovely Halekulani (holly-koo-la-knee) hotel at Waikiki beach. Mrs. Kimmel was on the Mainland because Kimmel wanted nothing to distract him from his job. The admiral had his usual single drink before dinner and left the party about 9:30 p.m.

His opposite number in the army, Lieutenant General Walter C. Short, Commander of the Hawaiian Department, and Mrs. Short went to a cocktail party at the home of friends, then to a charity dinner-dance at Schofield Barracks, the army's big infantry base. Like Kimmel, the Shorts went home early. The general and the admiral had a date to play golf Sunday morning.

Lieutenant Sam Brown, senior aviator on the heavy cruiser *New Orleans*, was home nursing a strep throat. He and his wife, Anne, had just moved into a rented home near the *Waialae* (wy-a-lie) Golf Club, near the shore "out Koko Head" way, or east of Honolulu beyond Waikiki and Diamond Head. Anne was worried because it cost $100 a month furnished, a lot on a navy lieutenant's pay.

Sam felt so lousy that they had turned down an invitation to dine that evening on the battleship *Arizona* at its berth in Pearl Harbor with Annapolis classmate Lieutenant George Pittard and his wife, Sally.

There was no party that night for Jim Gray, the previous occupant of the Brown's new home. Also a navy lieutenant, Jim was a pilot in *Fighting Six*, the fighter squadron on the carrier *Enterprise*. The Big E was at sea, en route home from delivering 12 new F4F fighter planes and their pilots to the Marines on Wake Island.

Jim's wife, Peggy, and their infant daughter, Dougie, were at sea, too. They had sailed from Honolulu Friday on the liner *Lurline* for San Francisco because Jim believed that war in the Pacific was near. If it came, he did not want them to be in Honolulu while he was at sea most of the time.

For Francis McCarthy, a United Press correspondent, it was party night. Mac was en route from UP's headquarters in New York to a new assignment in Manila. He had been bumped off a Pan American flight three days earlier to make room for, as Mac put it, "a load of tires." The tires were for allied aircraft in Southeast Asia.

Also bumped off the plane with Mac was a young man in army suntans without insignia. I met him with Mac at the Young Hotel bar in downtown Honolulu. "I'm Lieutenant Frank Baumer, U.S. Army Air Corps, retired," he grinned as he shook my hand, "and these are my orders. . . ."

He was one of a number of young army fliers who had been detached from active duty so they could go to Southeast Asia to fly with General Clair Chennault's "volunteer" *Flying Tigers*--for whom the tires probably were destined also.

Anyway, not knowing how soon he might be on his way to Manila again, Mac was determined to party Saturday night. By early evening he had a couple of charming Pan Am stewardesses in tow and was headed for dinner and dancing at Lau Yee Chai's. But he needed a man for the second stewardess so he called Captain Harry Albright, former newspaperman and army reserve, now on active duty at Fort Shafter as press relations officer in the G-2 (Intelligence) section of the Hawaiian Department.

Harry had a date to go horseback riding early Sunday morning and had already gone to bed. "No, thanks," Harry said. "If you won't meet us there, we're coming over and we'll drag you out of bed," Mac replied.

Harry laughed that off but he didn't know McCarthy very well. In a few minutes Mac arrived at Harry's house with the girls, so Harry gave in, got up and dressed.

Meanwhile, Kay and I were guests at a black tie dinner-dance at the officers club at Fort De Russey, an army post at Waikiki beach. Our hosts were Commander George Gelley, Coast Guard Chief of Staff in Hawaii, and his wife, Peggy, friends almost since our arrival in Honolulu.

De Russey was a cluster of low buildings bordering a large lawn which ended at a seawall above the western end of Waikiki beach.   Late in the evening, George and I strolled across the lawn and stood at the seawall. It was a typical balmy Hawaiian evening, the moon a few days past full. Some distance behind us, the dance floor, open to the lawn, was filled with ladies in evening gowns in the arms of officers in white mess jackets or civilians in white dinner jackets. The sound of music was gentle along the shore.

"I wonder what that is," I said as some faint flashes flickered far off on the southwestern horizon.

"There's no firing practice scheduled tonight," said George. We watched in silence for a few minutes, wondering about those faint flickers. Probably just heat lightning.

We were totally unaware of the storm gathering in the opposite direction where a huge Japanese naval force of six aircraft carriers and supporting battleships, cruisers and destroyers was moving into position. Aboard the carriers, the pilots of more than 350 fighters, divebombers and torpedo planes were preparing for the biggest assignment of their lives.

"It's like the calm before the storm," George said as we walked back toward the dancers.

As was our custom, Kay and I stopped at a small Japanese food stand on the way home for a late night snack—*saimin* and *yaki nikku*, noodle soup and meat-on-a-stick.

At home we tumbled quickly into bed, Kay not even bothering to put away her new evening dress. She just hung it on a wire hanger in the open bedroom door.

But the party wasn't over for Mac, definitely not a party-pooper. When the dancing stopped at midnight at Lau Yee Chai's, he insisted on carrying it elsewhere. First stop was the home of Bill Hutchinson, a copy editor at the

Honolulu *Advertiser.* "Bill wasn't too happy to have us descending on him and his wife at that hour of the night," Albright commented later.

Harry left Mac and his girl at the Hutchinson's, took his date back to her hotel, went home and changed into his riding clothes and returned to pick up McCarthy. "Mac still would not go home," Harry said, electing instead to pay a visit to Bill and Beth Tyree who lived in Waikiki. Bill was my assistant in the UP bureau, one of the best reporters and fastest, smoothest writers I ever knew.

At the Tyrees' they found Denny Smith and her husband, Jack, an *Advertiser* reporter and, in post-war years, a columnist for the Los Angeles *Times.* Finally, sometime after dawn, Albright got McCarthy, his date and the Smiths into his old car and headed downtown.

Suddenly they heard heavy gunfire but they thought it was from navy ships engaged in firing practice at sea. Then, about halfway into town, abreast of radio station KGMB, they became aware of a very large airplane flying low overhead. "It was one of our B-17's looking for a place to land," Albright said, referring to a flight of 12 Flying Fortresses which had taken off Saturday night from Hamilton Field near San Francisco on the first leg of a flight to the Philippines.

"I thought this was very strange. Then I noticed a lot of black splotches in the sky above Pearl Harbor. It still didn't register on me what really was happening.

"When I got McCarthy and his date to the old Young hotel to have breakfast, we could hear sirens whining here and there while a great cloud of smoke was rising into the air over Hickam Field and Pearl.

"I immediately thought that an ammunition dump had blown and knew, inasmuch as I was in charge of army press relations, that I had better get to Shafter.

"I put the gas to the floor and made the fastest run to Shafter I've ever made. Running up the stairs to the G-2 Section at the Headquarters building, I met Colonel Kendall Fielder (G-2 chief) in proper uniform. He was very calm. " 'There must be a war on,' I said. " 'If you will be quiet, you can hear it,' he replied."

2: "Flash -- Pearl Harbor Under Attack

"Frank, why are you walking on my dress?"

Anger sounded in Kay's sleepy mumble from the nearby bed. She was oblivious to the crack of anti-aircraft fire and some heavier booms in the distance.

The antiaircraft fire had aroused me minutes earlier, and drawn me to the front windows of our hillside home above Honolulu. To the right about eight airline miles away lay Pearl Harbor, partially hidden by Red Hill in the mid-distance. Above the navy yard, a few black puffs of anti-aircraft smoke blossomed. My watch said 7:58 a.m.

"Odd time for another drill," I thought as I padded barefoot and nude back toward the bedroom. But the noise intensified and I turned back to the windows. Now a tower of black smoke arose slowly from the area of the navy yard beyond Red Hill. An errant antiaircraft shell in the oil tank farm?

I rushed back to the bedroom to the phone at the foot of the bed, knocking Kay's dress from the hanger in the doorway as I passed.

I dialed the number of Lieutenant Buck Riddick, 14th Naval District Public Information Officer, who lived at Makalapa Heights above the harbor. No answer. I dialed

9

another number.   Lieutenant Forrest Allen, Buck's assistant, answered.

"What's going on out there?" I asked.

"I don't know but all hell's breaking loose," Allen said. "Buck's gone down to the yard to check."

Back to the front windows. Far to the left, Diamond Head rose peacefully beyond Waikiki.   Below me, Honolulu seemed to doze in the morning sunlight. But to the right, over Pearl, the tower of black smoke now was a billowing mass. The air was full of antiaircraft puffs and more smoke clouds began to rise from the Navy Yard.

Back at the phone, I tried Lieutenant Commander Waldo Drake, Pacific Feet PIO. Again no answer so I dialed G-2 at Fort Shafter.   Harry Albright answered.

"Do you know what's happening?" I asked.

"We're under attack but the planes aren't identified," he said. "You don't think they're Germans, do you?" I asked sarcastically as I hung up.

With international telephone service slow and Mackay Radio, RCA and Globe Wireless all closed on Sundays, my next call was to the Commercial Cable Company.

"Urgent Unipress Sanfrancisco, Newyork Manila, "I dictated.   "Flash Pearl Harbor under aerial attack. Tremaine."

A *flash* is the highest priority on news service wires, reserved for use only on a world-shaking story.

Then I placed a phone call to the United Press bureau in San Francisco via the international operator. In those days, long before long distance direct dialing, I had little hope that it would get through very quickly but it was worth a try.

Then I got back to Albright. "We can say now it's the Japs," he said.   He had no information as to damage or casualties. Another urgent cable to San Francisco, New York and Manila.

A call to Allen confirmed the attack but he had few more specifics. By this time, Kay was up and watching from the front windows after handing me my robe. I sent more urgent cables with descriptions of what she could see.

Meanwhile, Tyree had gotten through to me. We agreed that he would go to our office in the Honolulu *Advertiser* building, which was closer to his end of town, to coordinate our reporting with that of the *Advertiser* staff. He already had talked to McCarthy and Mac was trying to get to Shafter. That was on my way to Pearl Harbor so I told Bill I'd meet Mac at Shafter, then go on to the navy yard.

I also asked Bill to be sure that Dick Richards, whose radio receiving station handled our incoming service for local clients, was on the job even though service normally did not start until noon on Sundays.

Meanwhile, Kay had turned on the radio.

"Take cover. This is an air raid. This is no drill." It was the voice of Webley Edwards, manager of radio station KGMB and later a CBS radio correspondent.

He repeated the warning over and over, interspersing it with instructions for all army, navy, and Marine Corps, police, civil defense workers and Red Cross personnel to report to their posts immediately.

As I threw on some clothes, I went over with Kay the notes I had made on my phone calls and the cables I'd sent.

"If that call gets through to SX (San Francisco bureau), dictate from these notes and tell them anything else you can see," I said. "Tell them everything you can."

I gave her a hug and and dashed to the car. As I went out the door, I could hear Edwards repeating again and again, "Take cover. This is an air raid. This is no drill."

3 :   Peaceful Hawaii

Kay and I experienced our first practice alert the day
we arrived in Honolulu in June 1940 on the liner *Matsonia*.
She was my bride of nine months and I was a 26-year-old
newsman going on assignment, manager of the Honolulu
bureau of United Press.

The idea of running the news service's two-man bureau
in the *Paradise of the Pacific* was attractive from many
standpoints but, to an ambitious young newsman, even
with only four years experience, it seemed like a
backwater. It had taken some persuasion on the part of
my boss, Joe Jones, vice president in charge of the Foreign
Department, to convince me to accept.

I had been on the Foreign Desk in New York for nearly
a year and a half, editing service for our overseas clients
and operating in the tension surrounding the last days of
peace in Europe, the invasion of Poland, the British
evacuation from Dunkirk, the excitement of the early days
of World War II.

Leaving that for peaceful Hawaii, far removed from the
war in Europe and almost as far from the Japanese threat
to Southeast Asia and China, did not seem like a good
career move. But Joe convinced me that Honolulu was
only a stepping stone to Manila, Shanghai, Tokyo, where

the opportunities might be even greater than in Europe. He didn't mention Honolulu as a news center itself and I never considered that to be much of a possibility.

When Kay and I walked down the *Matsonia's* gangplank and through the steamship terminal under Aloha Tower, the first things we saw were machine guns in sandbag emplacements across the street, manned by steel-helmeted soldiers. That the helmets were old-fashioned World War I soup-plate variety should have indicated something about the state of Hawaii's readiness had I been perceptive enough to see it.

Anyway, a practice alert was on but, aside from having to wait for a convoy of military vehicles to pass, it did not delay us. Wendel Burch, the man I was replacing, and his wife, Laverne, had met us on the ship, draped lovely flower leis around our necks and now were driving us to our temporary quarters at the Halekulani hotel at Waikiki beach.

"You'll like the Halekulani," Laverne said. "It's just what you imagined Hawaii would be."

And so it was. We parked on a narrow side street and walked along the edge of a spacious lawn dotted with tall palm trees toward the two-story dark wooden main building. Its semi-open lobby ran through to a lovely lanai—an open patio—overlooking the beach where small waves broke gently on the sand. A balmy breeze wafted the fragrance of flowers into the lobby as we registered.

"They call this 'The hotel of the newlyweds and the nearlydeads'" our Hawaiian bellboy explained as he conducted us to our quarters, one of about a dozen bungalows bordering one side of the lawn. On the other side, facing the beach and partially hidden in the foliage, stood another low building.

"That's ' the House Without a Key,'" the bellboy said,

referring to the setting of one of Erle Stanley Gardner's most famous mystery stories.

The Halekulani seemed to deserve its reputation. It was a beautiful introduction to Hawaii and most of its guests did seem to be young couples on their honeymoons or older couples, perhaps enjoying second honeymoons. But our transfer expense account permitted only three days of such luxury living so Kay had to get busy.

While she tried to find permanent quarters which we could afford on a young newsman's salary, I got acquainted with the area and my responsibilities. She finally located what proved to be an ideal location, not only for living but for the events which came later so unexpectedly.

It was a small cottage on the old Trent estate about halfway up *Alewa* (ah-lev-ah) Heights, a residential area on the side of a high ridge, part of the mountain range which rose behind the city. After finding it, Kay hurried downtown to the bureau.

"You've got to see this," she said excitedly, and dragged me off to look at it.

As we entered the circular driveway from the street past a screen of foliage on the right, we passed a parking area in front of a four-car garage with a two-bedroom apartment above it, a swimming pool screened by a high hedge, then a two-story, two-unit guest cottage built down the side of the steep hill. The drive then circled left along the edge of the hill looking out toward Honolulu and the sea, then left again past the stately white main residence and back to the street. The driveway encircled a sizeable lawn.

What she had found for us was the top deck of the guest cottage which was reached from the driveway by a narrow wooden footbridge shaded by coconut palms and a big mango tree. Winding stone steps meandered down the side of the hill toward a rectangular fish pond and covered lanai on the left and the door to the first floor unit on the right.

Our apartment consisted of a bedroom, bathroom, kitchen and a large L-shaped living room and dining area. The two sides of the living-dining area were composed entirely of wide windows rising from knee-height to the ceiling. The sweeping view was spectacular—from Diamond Head far to our left, past the city and harbor of Honolulu dead ahead, then along the coast to Pearl Harbor and far beyond. When the Japanese struck, it was fortuitous as well.

The $55 a month it cost, furnished, seemed like a lot but we couldn't pass it up.

The Honolulu bureau was responsible for receiving and processing UP's incoming news report for the morning Honolulu *Advertiser,* the evening Honolulu *Star-Bulletin*, the Japanese-English *Hawaii Hochi,* radio station KGMB and for relaying an abbreviated service to clients on the islands of Kauai, Hawaii and Maui. We also, theoretically at least, were responsible for covering news of anything that might happen in the Pacific from Hawaii to Asia and the Philippines in the west and from the Aleutians in the north to as far south as one could imagine.

Actually, of course, we seldom heard from anywhere in our area outside of Hawaii although we did have a correspondent on Pitcairn Island far to the south where descendants of the survivors of Captain Bligh's *Bounty* still lived. Once a year, when a ship made its annual call there, our man sent UP a letter summarizing the year's events on Pitcairn—hardly headline news but sometimes worth a feature story. Had I been a stamp collector, I might have known that the stamps on the envelope probably were worth more than the copy.

In those days, long before satellite communications, transoceanic news service was delivered by commercial cable or radio at costly per-word rates or by less expensive blind radio transmissions called beamcasts. In the latter, Press Wireless, Inc., a press communications company, would relay copy from a news service to Press Wireless' own or client receiving stations on pre-arranged schedules. The receivers had no direct communication back to the transmitter so if electrical disturbances in the atmosphere or other problems prevented reception, there was no way to get a repeat except to send a commercial message requesting a special transmission.

In the case of Hawaii, our competitors, the Associated Press and International News Service, received condensed reports via the more expensive but more reliable per word service. United Press received more voluminous, although still skimpy, reports on beamcasts from Press Wireless' transmitter in San Francisco to the Press Wireless receiving station near Honolulu for 60-word-per-minute teletype relay to our office.

Shortly after I arrived, Press Wireless announced that it would close its Honolulu receiving station. It would continue the transmissions from San Francisco, if UP wanted them, but it was up to us to arrange our own reception. This was a major dilemma for an inexperienced young bureau manager. I could see disaster looming in our relationship with our Hawaiian clients because our service rates and volume commitments were based on the beamcast system.

After several weeks of sleepless nights and days of futile effort, I finally located a former commercial radio operator named Dick Richards who had a new wife and an ambition to get into business for himself. We negotiated a deal for him to take over the Press Wireless' receiving station and responsibility for recording radio news for us.

In fact, he soon taught wife Elsa to handle radio receptions, too, and thus expanded our service by picking up UP beamcasts meant for other parts of the world as well. This increased our service from about 3,500 words per day to 15,000 or more, a real bonus for our Honolulu clients as the world crisis grew worse and worse.

On December 7, when the navy shut off all commercial communications to and from Hawaii they somehow overlooked Dick's receiving set-up. So for three days, UP was Hawaii's only source of information from the outside world except for people with radios which could pick up the 50,000 watt stations in Los Angeles and San Francisco.

Life in Honolulu in 1940 and '41 was close to idyllic for a couple of young newlyweds. We often commented about it to new-found friends and the standard reply was, "Oh, but you should have seen it before all the defense workers came."

It was true that there was a new element in town. Thousands of people had arrived to work on the expanding facilities at Pearl Harbor, the big army air base at Hickam Field, the Kaneohe Naval Air Station and elsewhere. The new arrivals strained the city's housing and their cars crowded its streets.

Rentable houses were hard to find and the traffic problem became so serious that a system of one-way streets was instituted in the downtown area for the first time in Honolulu's history. The military developed several major projects to relieve the housing problem at Pearl Harbor and the adjacent Hickam Field. Between them they became the third largest concentration of population in the territory after the cities of Honolulu and Hilo on the "Big Island" of Hawaii.

In a UP dispatch early in December 1941, I wrote, "Peaceful Hawaii — with big guns booming, warplanes droning overhead and defense works springing up like magic—is taking on the attributes of a war capital and a boom defense town, but the situation is neither as acute nor romantically dangerous as some reports recently circulated on the Mainland would indicate.. . . .

"The big guns of Hawaii's coast artillery and the batteries of the fleet often are heard in practice firing which rattles the windows and dishes of Honolulu homes. War planes are so common in the Hawaiian skies that only the visitor of a few days bothers to look up as they roar past.

"Several nights a week, searchlight beams stab the sky as anti-aircraft defenses are put through practice paces. Pearl Harbor, the giant fleet base, Schofield Barracks, the huge army post, and other army and navy centers often stage practice blackouts while the whole territory blacked out under simulated air raid conditions one night last summer. It is not unusual to see steel-helmeted and armed soldiers standing guard at bridges and vital installations at various points in the Islands as the army has been on a more or less continual 'alert' for more than a year.

"Residents of Hawaii take all this and the discomforts caused by overcrowding as a result of the influx of huge numbers of defense workers as part of the situation necessary to the present world situation.

"Local residents are not much worried about what Japanese-Americans in the Islands will do and, on the basis of oft-repeated statements by high army and navy officials here, the military services are convinced of the loyalty of a majority of Hawaiian Japanese-Americans."   All were displeased because Congress was considering a bill sponsored by the War Department which would give the president the power to declare martial law in Hawaii and Puerto Rico whenever a state of emergency exists or invasion threatens. They pointed out that Hawaii recently had passed its own "M-Day" bill which gave the governor, an appointee of the president, almost dictatorial powers in an emergency including the power to declare martial law.

But despite all this, it still was Hawaii where you went to work in an open neck, short-sleeved aloha shirt, where the nights were balmy and where the uncrowded beaches—when you got away from Waikiki—were great for picnics, day or night.

The fact that on some of our picnics with friends in the navy, we played war games among the sand dunes didn't really bring home to us the threat of war in our own little part of heaven.

4: Bedlam

As I snaked the car through the curves down Alewa Drive, my back to the Pearl Harbor area, it seemed like any peaceful Sunday morning. Even though I could hear sirens in the distance, hardly anyone was up in our neighborhood and the homes basked quietly in the sun, most of them partially hidden behind lush Hawaiian foliage.

To my left, some clouds hung low over the green mountains of the Koolau (Ko-oh-low) range. Down below, however, I began to see more people. As I came out of Alewa Drive, I faced toward Pearl Harbor again and the black smoke towered higher and higher. On those back streets, the houses were closer together and more people stood in their yards, all looking into the sky. Some still were in their nightclothes.

The scream of sirens was louder here but their wail and Web's warning, "Take cover. This is an air raid," didn't seem to register with them.

Downtown, McCarthy found a more hectic atmosphere when he emerged from the Young hotel.

"Bedlam," he wrote later. "Huge columns of smoke rising from Pearl Harbor. Mad screech of brakes as speeding cars missed each other, horns tooting.

"A Japanese plane soared lazily overhead, down under 1,000 feet. It banked slowly, and the Rising Sun was plain on its wings. I watched it out of sight.

"In the street, service men, some dressing as they ran, rushed for transportation to their posts. There were more planes in the air now. Civilians seemed dazed, gathering in small clusters. The din was incessant, the booms and cracks of anti-aircraft much louder."

In several parts of the city, including downtown, there were explosions, casualties and damage. Many people thought the Japanese were bombing the city but the explosions later proved to have been our own anti-aircraft shells which failed to explode in the air as they should have.

"I couldn't get transportation and started walking to Ft. Shafter," McCarthy continued. "The trip was a combined walk and hitchhike. The road was jammed with cars headed in both directions."

When I drove through the gate at Shafter, it was alive with activity. Ft. Shafter was not a fort at all as the average civilian visualizes one. As headquarters of the Army's Hawaiian Department, it was mostly a cluster of low administration buildings in a campus-like setting without fortifications, gun emplacements and the like. Now, GIs were hurriedly digging slit trenches and setting up machine gun emplacements.

I went directly to Albright's office where I found Harry and Colonel Fielder. Here there was ordered calm under Fielder's direction. "Fielder was superb," Harry said years later, recalling the shock and tension of the morning and the trying days immediately afterward. "He was the glue that held Hawaii together."

Mac arrived within minutes and we agreed that he should stay there at G-2, where whatever information the Army had would be gathered, while I would try to get to Pearl Harbor in my car.

By this time, every defense worker and military man on the island of Oahu was trying to get to his post, most of them at Pearl. Consequently, when I reached Dillingham Boulevard, the main route, a monstrous traffic jam had developed. In 1941, it was only a two-lane thoroughfare and the line of cars was just inching along.

Finally, I could stand it no longer. There was hardly any traffic in the inbound lane toward Honolulu, so I pulled out of line and drove as fast as I dared down the wrong side of the road. When I reached the gates at Hickam Field, not far from the entrance to the Navy Yard, I could see that I stood little chance of getting through that mess and into the Navy Yard anytime soon.

So, instead, I turned in at Hickam and sailed through the entrance with only a brief stop for the sentry. As I drove into the base, I could see that some residences had been hit, apparently by bomb fragments and machine gun bullets, but damage did not appear to be extensive at that point.

Then I rounded a curve and saw a wrecked barracks. It was a three-story stucco building badly damaged from bomb hits on its roof and resultant fires. There were many casualties there.

Looking westward, I could see the narrow entrance channel to Pearl Harbor beyond the Hickam fence. Several destroyers raced through it toward the sea in single file at high speed, evidence that the navy still was in operation at least. I could not look far enough into the Yard from my position, however, to see what was happening there and what the source of all the smoke was.

I found a phone and called Tyree with this information and told him I'd try to get into Pearl from Hickam. He suggested that I stay where I was because the *Advertiser* was getting reports from one of its circulation men who had been in the Yard when the attack started and he was picking that up.

I left the phone and walked out to the flight line. The wreckage of dozens of planes littered the edge of the field where the Japanese had found them bunched together for protection against sabotage. A hit on one plane wreaked havoc among others as fire spread from one to the next.

The wreckage included old B-18 bombers, new B-17 Flying Fortresses and a lot of fighters—P-40's and older P-36's. There must have been 50 or 60 of them at least, maybe more.

The hangars were a mess. Sunlight poured through great gaping holes in their roofs, walls were blown out and wreckage littered their interiors. The Honolulu Fire Department had joined Hickam's fire fighters in battling the flames. The air field's own firehouse had taken a direct hit which tore up the water mains, sent geysers of water into the air, and hampered the firefighting.

There were wrecked buildings all over the base. Casualties must have been heavy but nobody could guess then what they might be.

I didn't know it at the time, but in the midst of the Japanese attack, the 12 B-17's from Hamilton Field had arrived and come under attack as they made their landing approaches. In California they had been loaded heavily with fuel for the long flight instead of with ammunition and their guns had been stored in the bomb bays. Unarmed and with only skeleton crews, they were defenseless, but all but one of them survived, finding a spot to land at Hickam or elsewhere on Oahu.

I had called Tyree several times with information as I collected it. After one call, as I stepped outside the building from which I had phoned, a lone Jap plane swooped in from the direction of Pearl, machine guns blazing. Two air corps men and I dived for the doorway and I received my only injury of the war—a moccasin-shod big toe badly trampled by an airman's boot.

A little after 11 a.m., I phoned Tyree again. "Save it," he said. "You might as well come in with anything else you have. The navy has shut down all communications."

As I drove back toward Honolulu, I wondered what was in store for us and how we had done on this big story, the biggest of our careers. In hot news service competition, a reporter generally sees the opposition at work but I had not yet seen an AP man nor the part-time correspondent who represented INS.

Later I learned that we had done very well indeed. My cables had gotten through quickly, ahead of anyone else's, even though the White House announcement of the attack beat them by a few minutes. The phone call I had placed was completed shortly after I left home and Kay had handled it masterfully, giving UP a great eye-witness account.

At Shafter after I left, Mac had picked up a phone on an unmanned desk and placed a call to the San Francisco bureau. Since it was an official line, he got through immediately and started dictating. He kept the phone open, relaying information as he was able to collect it there in the G-2 office.

The operator interrupted from time to time to ask if Mac was on an official call. He would simply say, "I am phoning from G-2 at Fort Shafter." That satisfied her for a while but she finally got wise and cut him off.

Downtown at our bureau, Tyree had filed by phone and cable from my reports to him and material from the *Advertiser* staff, so we had gotten out quite a lot of information before the navy shut everyone off.

My first cables had been dual-filed both to the States

and to Manila because we also were responsible for providing Asia direct with news from our area. Three years later, Frank Hewlett, who had been UP manager in Manila, joined my staff in the South Pacific.

"You remember that flash you sent from Pearl Harbor?" he said. "When I received it, I phoned the office of Admiral Hart (Commander in Chief, Asiatic Fleet). The guy on duty said, 'Bunk. Tell your Pearl Harbor correspondent to go back to bed and sleep it off.' When I phoned back with your next bulletin," Frank said, "he had the word from Washington."

5: No Time For Tears   (Kay)

When Frank went out the door, I wondered if our kiss would be our last.

But there was no time for tears. I turned toward the bedroom to pick up my crumpled dress. It was a beautiful tulle and sequin creation from I. Magnin in Los Angeles, a recent gift from my mother. Would I ever wear it again?

Last night had been so beautiful. While Frank and George chatted out by the sea wall, Peggy and I sat in the pale light on the lawn near the open dance floor. The music was sweet and soft. It seemed so peaceful.

When Frank and George returned, it was close to midnight and the dance was nearly over. Even though there were lots of them, most parties ended early in Hawaii. Frank took me in his arms as the band played the lovely "Aloha Oe" with its haunting refrain"... until we meet again." I thought how lucky we were to have been sent to this beautiful place so early in our young married lives.

When we got home after our Japanese snack, I was tired. I should have hung my beautiful dress in the closet on a proper hanger but, instead, I just slipped it over a dry cleaner's wire hanger, hung it in the doorway to the bedroom and followed Frank into bed.

26

That was the last thing I knew until the next morning when I felt him crawl over me from his side of the bed next to the wall. He bumped me and pulled our light blanket off my shoulders. That irritated me but I tried to go back to sleep.

Then I heard him moving back and forth from the bedroom to the living room. I opened my eyes slightly, just little slits.

"For gosh sakes, what on earth are you doing?" I asked. No answer.

Then, to my horror, he came rushing back from the living room, not even in his bathrobe, and stepped right on my dress which was lying on the floor. He must have knocked it down earlier. Now he was walking on it. He made me so furious sometimes.

"Why are you walking on my dress?" I muttered. All I really wanted to do was go back to my pleasant dreams. I was angry but I was trying not to wake up. He didn't answer. I could hear him dialing the telephone which sat on a ledge on the wall at the foot of the bed.

"You can't say who it is?" I heard him say. "You don't think it's the Germans, do you?" That got my attention.

He dialed another number. It must have been the cable company because I heard him dictate a message addressed to United Press.

"Flash," he said. "Pearl Harbor under aerial attack."

I jumped out of bed and ran to the front windows myself. There was a huge cloud of black smoke coming up in the direction of Pearl Harbor. I turned on the radio, then got Frank his robe.

On the radio, I could hear our friend Webley Edwards at KGMB saying, "This is an air raid. Take cover. This is an air raid. This is no drill."

Frank made some more phone calls, sent some more messages, then threw on his clothes, telling me all the while

27

what to do if the phone call he had placed to San Francisco came through.

The kiss, the hug, then he sprinted across the footbridge and I was left there alone. The ominous boom of explosions and the sharper sound of antiaircraft fire seemed louder now.

When I'm nervous or upset, I try to stay busy so I got to work. After picking up my dress and hanging it in the closet, I filled the bathtub with water. That was in case the water service went out or the water became contaminated. Next I stripped the sheets and pillow cases from the beds, got the towels from the bathroom and kitchen and stuffed them into the dirty clothes bag along with the clothing already there.

All the time I could hear Web telling service men, defense workers, policemen, firemen, Red Cross workers to go to their posts and repeating his warning, "Take cover. This is an air raid. This is no drill."

Then he added something. "This is the real McCoy," he said. I guess some people hadn't believed him.

I carried the bag up to the garage where the laundry room was located and dumped everything into the washing machine. The machines of those days were pretty primitive compared with those we have now. They were automatic, but not very.

I dumped in the clothes, turned on the water, added soap chips, waited for the water to reach the proper level, turned it off and started the machine. The automatic part was that the agitator would turn itself off after the desired period of time. Then you were supposed to return to start the drain and rinse operations and, finally, run the clothes through the wringer.

Well, I set the timer for the agitator, then returned to the house, expecting to come back soon to finish the job.

The next time I saw those clothes, or even thought of them, was three days later. They were still sitting there in the cold, soapy water.

As I walked back along the driveway toward the footbridge, I could see a destroyer at sea off Honolulu harbor directly in front of me. A plane circled above it. I walked to the brow of the hill to watch. The plane appeared to be attacking the destroyer because intermittent geysers of water flew up all around it, but I saw no hits. The ship fired back, but the plane, too, apparently escaped damage and finally flew away.

The action was too far away for me to distinguish any markings but it had to be a Japanese plane attacking an American destroyer. I learned later that the ship was the USS *Ward* on patrol duty. It actually had discovered, attacked and sunk a Japanese sub off the entrance to Pearl Harbor about 7 a.m. but its report failed to alert the navy to what was about to happen.

I turned and went back to the house. A few minutes later, Sam and Anne Brown drove in, parked in the driveway and came running across the bridge. Sam was a navy lieutenant, senior aviator on the cruiser *New Orleans*.

"We tried to call but your line was busy," Sam said. "I've got to get to the ship. Can Anne stay here?"

"Of course," I said, and Sam kissed Anne and ran back to his car.

I had to laugh at Anne. In fact, we laughed a lot at each other. I guess that's why we liked each other so much.

The reason this time was what she had brought with her. No clothes, not even a nightgown. No toothbrush, no toilet articles. What she had grabbed when she and Sam dashed out of their house out beyond Diamond Head was a carton of cokes and a book entitled, *A Woman Faces the War*.

29

"Well, the water might get contaminated," said Anne, explaining the cokes. The book was by an English woman who had lived through the bombing of London. Made sense to me.

"They warned on the radio that we ought to evacuate the beach areas in case they try to invade," Anne said. "Sam thought that Frank, being a newsman, probably would know before most people what's going on."

Years later, she gave me another reason. "You taught me how to peel potatoes and look for the Thursday specials in the newspaper ads," she explained. "We thought you were very secure people."

Well, from my vast experience of nine months as a housewife when we had first met, I had taught Anne a few things about the kitchen and keeping the household bills down. She had been a brand new bride a year and a half earlier when she and Sam, Frank and I had all come out to Honolulu together on the *Matsonia*.

We went out across the bridge to the driveway and lawn to see if we could get a better view of what was happening. As we watched the smoke pouring into the sky from Pearl Harbor, we were joined by Sue Davidson, our neighbor in the garage apartment, and her sister, Mary Burkhardt.

Sue's husband, Bob, was an ensign on the mine sweeper *Sothard*, a converted old four-stack destroyer which later became famous as the model for the USS *Caine* in Herman Wouk's book, *The Caine Mutiny*. Mary, who was visiting from the mainland, was engaged to Don Goodrich, an ensign on the light cruiser *Detroit*.

Up the steps from the apartment below came Ruth Iverson and her two-and-a-half year old daughter, Lovice. Ruth was worried about her husband, a destroyer skipper, who was at sea on his ship. Sue was upset because it was hers and Bob's wedding anniversary and, of course, he had dashed off as soon as the radio told them what was happening.

As we watched, I heard the telephone ring in our apartment. I ran inside to answer.

"I have San Francisco on the line," the operator said. On the other end was Jim Sullivan in the UP bureau there. I quickly read him the notes Frank had left and told him about all the smoke over Pearl Harbor and the antiaircraft fire and about the fight I had seen between the destroyer and the attacking plane.

Then I heard a screaming noise, becoming more intense. It was a sort of siren-like whistle such as I had heard in war movies when bombs were falling. I suddenly realized that the noise was not a Hollywood invention at all but the real thing.

I stood there, telephone in hand, wondering if this was my last moment. Then there was a loud explosion, so loud that I thought it must have been right there on the estate.

"Good Lord," I gasped. Then, "I'm still alive."

"What was that?" said Jim.

The screaming noise and the explosion were so loud that he could hear the whole thing back there in San Francisco. It really added something to the story.

I told Jim to wait while I ran outside to see what had happened. The anti-aircraft shell—for that's what it later proved to be—had hit about 50 yards from our house on the side of the hill on which the estate was located. Nobody was hurt and there was no damage except for a small crater in the side of the hill, but a shell fragment had grazed the forehead of a man standing nearby.

I learned later that many of our own anti-aircraft shells, apparently improperly fused, had fallen in various parts of Honolulu, in some cases causing deaths, injuries and fires. I reported back to Jim and he rang off.

Pearl Harbor

Our close call had made all of us "temporary widows" very nervous. Suddenly, we all had to go to the bathroom. I don't know why we all lined up in our house for our one bathroom instead of using Ruth's and Susie's, too. A desire for togetherness, I guess.

While I was waiting for my turn, I suddenly realized that nobody had eaten anything yet. The morning was wearing on and we should have something in our stomachs. That led me to one of the wisest things I did all day—egg-nogs.

Fortunately, I had the makings. We always had eggs and milk in the house but normally, on our income, we didn't stock much booze. On this occasion, however, we happened to have a pretty good supply because, when our friend Peggy Gray was closing her house to leave on the *Lurline,* she had sold me the liquor she and Jim had left over. At officer's club prices, that was a bargain that this civilian couldn't turn down.

So I threw together a batch of egg-nogs and that settled us all down. The milk and eggs satisfied our hunger and the whiskey calmed our nerves. Nothing could really calm our fears, however. Where were our husbands, what had happened to them? What was going to happen to us? It was going to be a long day.

6: Not In My Nightgown!

A few minutes before 8 a.m., Pete Willett, the 12-year-old son of a naval officer quartered on Ford Island, emerged from his house to feed his rabbits in the back yard. Dad was away but his mother and teen-age sister, Edith, were inside, just getting up.

Ford Island was the Naval Air Station in the middle of Pearl Harbor, home of a squadron of patrol planes. It also housed planes from carriers and scout planes from heavy cruisers and battleships when they were in port.

At the north end of Ford Island's eastern shore lay Battleship Row and from his yard, about 150 yards away, Pete could see the *Nevada* and *Arizona* in a single file at the top of the row. The repair ship *Vestal* lay just outboard of the *Arizona*. Hidden from his view, lying two abreast, were the *Tennessee* and *West Virginia*, *Maryland* and *Oklahoma*, then the tanker *Neosho* and finally the *California*.

Across the channel was the Submarine Base building where Admiral Kimmel had his headquarters.

Suddenly planes began diving at the island. Pete saw an explosion and flames. "Then I heard this noise and looked to the left," Pete said. "Here came 30 to 40 planes very low over the submarine base. They were in perfect wing tip to wing tip formation and I was fascinated. One went down the street in front of the quarters, one-story buildings, so low that it disappeared behind the house.

"It came out the other side, and on its side was a great big red ball staring me in the face and right above it this guy shooting a machine gun. By then, everything was exploding. Only then did I realize it was the Japs.

"I ran across the street yelling, 'It's the Japs, it's the Japs', to the door of the commandant of the Station, Captain [James H.] Shoemaker. They had a Chinese cook who was standing at the kitchen door. I was so scared that I ran right through the screen yelling, 'Japs, Japs, Japs.' Shoemaker was sitting on his bed in his skivvies. He almost knocked me down getting out the door."

Shoemaker, still only in his skivvies, jumped into his car and roared out of the driveway, so reckless in his haste to get to his station that he knocked down his own mailbox at the corner of the driveway.

When he reached the administration building near the seaplane parking area, he found most of the planes wrecked or burning and the nearby hangars in flames.

Meanwhile, young Willett had scampered back across the street from Shoemaker's to his own house. Armed Marine guards already were pounding on front doors along the street, yelling instructions to dependents to assemble at the "Admiral's Dungeon," an old gun emplacement beneath the quarters of Rear Admiral Pat Bellinger, Commander of the Fleet's patrol wings.

Willett's sister Edith was in the shower and her mother was waiting. Mrs. Willett dismissed the young Marine at her door, saying, "Young man, I'm not going to be taken prisoner in my nightgown."

Meanwhile, the fatally stricken *Arizona* was exploding

and burning. Screaming divebombers and water-hugging torpedo bombers also had inflicted heavy damage on the other battleships along The Row and there were many fires.

Instead of taking cover, Willet and Captain Shoemaker's 16-year-old son watched in fascination, then decided they should do something. They found a rowboat and put off in it to join other small craft trying to help survivors from the *Arizona* and other ships.

"We had some friends on the *Arizona*," Pete said. "We made several trips out to take people back. We took two off the deck but it got too hot, so we picked others out of the water. There was so much oil on the surface that it gummed up their eyes. We had to scoop it away when we got them into the rowboat." Before long, some sailors took over from the boys and continued the rescue effort.

"After the attack ended," Pete said, "we were split up. Mother was at the administration building in charge of finding places for dependents on the island to stay. Edith was at an emergency ward at the BOQ (Bachelor Officers Quarters) helping take care of the wounded and I was at a machine gun emplacement helping carry ammunition."

7: In the Newsrooms

Riley Allen, the dedicated and meticulous editor of the Honolulu *Star-Bulletin*, went to his office most Sunday mornings and this was no exception. He had a reputation for reading every word that went into his paper so he spent a lot of hours there. Sunday morning was a good time for the busy editor of an afternoon newspaper to catch up on other work.

Suddenly his windows rattled. Almost automatically, he reached for the phone and dialed the number of his city editor, Howard Case.

"Howard, there's been a tremendous explosion out toward Pearl Harbor," Allen said. "Call Bading and get him on it right away."

"Where I lived in Waikiki, everything was calm and peaceful," Case wrote later. "The old mullet fishermen were patiently holding their long bamboo poles over the still waters of the Ala Wai (A-la-wy) Canal, and only a few people were stirring as it was only 8 o'clock and nearly everybody was sleeping in."

That included John Bading, the Star-Bulletin's military reporter, whose first reaction when Case called him was anger. But he told Case, "Okay, I'll start checking." Case hung up. Immediately, the phone rang again. "Howard, the Japs are bombing Pearl Harbor," a woman's voice said. "I didn't know then and I don't know now who she was," Case said. Her voice was unfamiliar, and after that one sentence, she hung up.

As Case threw on some clothes and prepared to leave for the office, there was a whistling sound and a loud crack as a shell landed near his home in the heart of Waikiki. It was another of the many American antiaircraft shells that failed to explode in the air and landed in the city.

Downtown, he parked his car and ran across the street toward the *Star-Bulletin*.

"I heard a plane overhead and looked up to see the two red balls on the wings of a Japanese plane as it headed toward Pearl Harbor," Case said. "I watched the antiaircraft fire but it all seemed to be underneath the attacking Japanese planes."

Over at the Honolulu *Advertiser,* the situation was different. A morning paper, its presses had broken down Saturday night while running the Sunday morning paper. They were still down on Sunday and the staff which gathered to cover the biggest story in the paper's history was frustrated beyond measure.

Finally, arrangements were made to run off an extra on the presses of the Hawaii *Hochi*, one of Honolulu's two bilingual newspapers, late in the afternoon.

8: Praise the Lord and Pass the Ammunition

On the heavy cruiser *New Orleans*, in drydock for engine repair across the channel from Battleship Row, it was almost time for church. Lieutenant Howell M. Forgy, the chaplain, a burly 220 pounder who had played football for Muskingum College in Ohio, was directing sailors erecting a heavy canvas canopy over the boat deck where he would conduct the service.

Suddenly, Japanese aircraft appeared, first dive bombers attacking the Naval Air Station on Ford Island across the way, then more dive bombers and torpedo bombers wreaking havoc along Battleship Row.

As General Quarters sounded on the *New Orleans*, Forgy dashed into the nearby galley, grabbed a meat cleaver and slashed the lashings holding up the canopy. As it collapsed on the deck, he rushed off to his battle station. There he found the power off on the nearby powder hoist which was supposed to lift heavy shells from the magazine below to the five-inch guns above, for even these unlikely weapons were in use against the enemy planes.

To overcome the problem, a gunnery officer, Lieutenant Edwin Woodhead, had organized a line of sailors to pass the ammunition by hand. Now, chaplains are not supposed to take part in combat and I never knew for sure whether Forgy jumped into the line, where his size and strength would have been a welcome addition, or whether he just stood by acting as a cheerleader.

At any rate, his religious instincts came to the fore and he began to chant over and over, "Praise the Lord and pass the ammunition, praise the Lord and pass the ammunition." The sailors joined in and the pace picked up as they served the guns with the big shells.

Thus was born the slogan that composer Frank Loesser soon turned into the song of the same name whose popularity lasted throughout World War Two!

9: "We Still Have Airplanes"

Out east near Waialae Golf Club "Koko Head way"—of Waikiki, Sam Brown stepped out of his house to see where all the planes were coming from.

"I looked up at a large formation of strange aircraft proceeding towards Pearl," Sam said. "Being an aviator, I knew they weren't American. I watched them for a while, then saw antiaircraft bursts over Pearl. Believe it or not, the first thought that crossed my mind was that the navy finally was having a realistic drill.

"I went back into the house and turned on the radio and my idea of a drill was quickly dispelled."

What he and Anne heard was the air raid warning and instructions to clear Waialae and other beach areas, prime targets if the Japanese attempted to land an invasion force.

Anne and Sam, who became a rear admiral in post-war days, had been among our closest friends in Hawaii so it didn't take them long to decide that Sam should drop Anne at our place en route to his ship.

When Sam reached the *New Orleans*, he found it undamaged "but a mess topside."

"Forgy's collapsed awning completely covered several of the five-inch guns and their crews," Sam said. "When I arrived, the gun crews still were trying to crawl out from under the awning and other men were trying to roll it up."

"We Still Have Airplanes"

The *New Orleans* had just received a new commanding officer but he was at sea on another cruiser doing a "make-you-learn" cruise, so the executive officer was acting C.O.

"I figured I better report to him to see if he had any orders for me as senior aviator of the four-seaplane cruiser unit, my planes then being parked on Ford Island," Sam said. "The exec was truly a spit-and-polish officer, very smart and good with the crew. He believed completely in the power of battleships and the battleline and had little use for aviators and their aircraft.

"After working my way around and under the collapsed awning, I finally reached the exec's cabin. Much to my surprise, he was pacing up and down, crying.

"I asked what was the matter and he said, 'We've lost the war, the battleline is sunk!' He could see Battleship Row through his cabin portholes.

"I said, 'Don't cry, Commander, we still have airplanes,' which made him cry even harder."

It seemed useless to Sam to remain there so he went ashore to try to reach Ford Island from the nearby Hospital Point landing.

"All the boats available were bringing the wounded and, I guess, the dead to this landing for transfer to the hospital nearby," Sam said. "It was a gruesome sight."

He bummed a ride in one of the boats returning to Ford Island and there found his four aircraft and three pilots relatively intact except that dirt, pieces of concrete and other debris from the bomb explosions had come down through the fabric of the planes' wings, the scout seaplanes being among the oldest aircraft still in service. "We found the next day that they flew about as well as they ever did in spite of the holes and collected dirt," Sam said.

As the four pilots contemplated their problems, another

scout plane settled onto the water nearby and started to taxi toward the seaplane ramp. Piloted by Lieutenant Mickey Reeves, it had been launched from a cruiser at sea with the *Enterprise* task force which was returning to base after delivering 12 new fighter planes to Marines on Wake Island.

Unaware of the Japanese attack, Reeves was coming in to pick up mail and the Sunday papers at Pearl. As he neared Oahu, he was jumped by two Japanese *Zeros*, fighter aircraft covering the Japanese bombers.

"In the ensuing dog fight," Sam related, "Mickey's plane had gotten a lot of holes through the floats, but in his slow old seaplane, he was able to out-turn the *Zeros* and all their bullets fortunately went low. The *Zeros* finally gave up trying to shoot Mickey down and proceeded out to sea."

Reeves then flew into Pearl and landed near the seaplane ramp where his plane normally would have been floated onto a dolly to be pulled ashore. In this case, however, the damaged floats quickly took in water and sank to the shallow bottom, stranding Reeves about 20 feet off shore. There he stayed until his friends ashore found a tractor with which they pulled the plane up the ramp.

10: Halsey Says "No!"

As the Japanese warplanes swept toward Oahu from the northwest that morning, the U.S. aircraft carrier *Enterprise* approached from the southwest. Her mission to deliver 12 new F4F fighter planes and their pilots to the Marines on Wake Island completed, the *Big E* and her escort of three heavy cruisers and nine destroyers was far over the horizon but approaching Barber's Point, the southwest corner of Oahu just west of Pearl Harbor.

The *Enterprise* task force under command of Rear Admiral William F. Halsey was far enough away not to be seen by the Japanese, nor were the Japanese detected by the Big E's dawn combat patrol which took off at 5:30 a.m.

The fact that the Pacific Fleet's three carriers were away from Pearl Harbor was one of the few fortunate things that happened to the navy that day.

The *Saratoga* was at the Navy Yard in Bremerton, Washington undergoing repairs. The *Lexington* had left Pearl Friday morning with the heavy cruisers *Chicago*, *Portland* and *Astoria* and five destroyers, bound for Midway

Island about 1,200 miles northwest of Oahu, well east of the Japanese launch point. The *Lex's* mission was to deliver 18 new fighter planes to the Marines at Midway Island.

Shortly after she left Pearl, the target ship *Utah*, an old battleship, had moved into her berth on the west side of Ford Island across from Battleship Row where the Japanese sank her.

The *Enterprise* and her task force had left Pearl on its mission on November 28. Not wanting to be slowed down by the three 17 knot battleships in his force, Halsey detached them and some support vessels shortly after leaving the harbor and sent them off on a routine training exercise.

With three heavy cruisers and nine destroyers, the *Enterprise*, capable of speeds of up to 30 knots, headed for Wake, 2,000 miles to the west. They were ready for whatever might come.

"The *Enterprise* is now operating under war conditions," Halsey told his men in his Battle Order No. 1. He ordered torpedoes armed with war heads, dive bombers with live bombs and he told the task force to sink any submarine and shoot down any airplane not known to be American.

"When we were near Wake, there was a contact report of Japanese ships which turned out to be false," Jim Gray said. Of course, Japan and the United States were not at war then so the task force should not have regarded such ships as enemy anyway, at least legally.

"Halsey covered that possibility," Gray said, "by signaling, 'If any Japanese are sighted, shoot them down in a friendly fashion.' "

After delivering the new fighters to the Wake Island Marines, the *Enterprise* task force headed back toward Pearl, her arrival there scheduled for Sunday morning. As dawn approached, the ships took their usual precautions.

"Dawn Combat Patrol launched at 0530 (5:30 a.m.)," the war diary of Fighting Squadron Six noted. "Scouting Six planes reported attack on Oahu by Japanese carrier group. Ship sounded General Quarters and announced War Plan 46 in effect against Japan. No planes launched to attack Japanese planes rendezvousing over Barber's Point."

Scouting Six was in a good position to report the attack. As was customary when approaching home port, the *Enterprise* had launched the squadron's 18 dive bombers for Ford Island while the task force still was about eight hours steaming time from home.

They arrived over Pearl Harbor as the first wave of Japanese planes was attacking. Jap fighters went after the unsuspecting Americans immediately. Even more disconcerting, their own anti-aircraft fired on them, too. The gunners had no idea that aircraft from the *Enterprise* were among those overhead.

The squadron skipper, Commander H.L. "Brig" Young, piloted Scouting Six's lead plane. Halsey's flag secretary, Lieutenant Commander Brum Nichol, was in the cockpit behind him.

As reported in Gordon W. Prange's book, *At Dawn We Slept*, Nichol's first thought was, "My God, the army has gone crazy having anti-aircraft drill on Sunday morning."

Then he saw the red balls on the planes around him. Young brought his plane through what Nichol described as "the damnedest amount of anti-aircraft fire and [machine gun] bullets I had ever seen, before or since" and landed at Ford Island.(1)

Of the 17 planes following Young, Japanese Zeros shot down four, American anti-aircraft got one, and a sixth crash-landed at an airfield on the neighboring island of Kauai.

The other 11 managed to elude the Japanese and get through our own anti-aircraft fire to land at Ford Island or the Marines' nearby *Ewa* (ehva) Field.

Back on the *Enterprise*, when Halsey received a message from CinCPac (Commander-in-Chief, Pacific) that Pearl Harbor was being attacked, he shouted, "My God, they're shooting down my own boys! Tell Kimmel!"(2)

Fighting Six's 18 fighters were on the flight deck, armed and with their engines running, ready to take off, hoping to get into the fight. Halsey cancelled their flight. Gray was sitting in the cockpit of his plane, eager to go. Squadron leader Lieutenant Commander Wade McCluskey climbed up onto the wing of Jim's plane. "Get him to launch us," Gray said. "We'll have a field day."

Whether they would have had a field day or not, outnumbered as they were, is questionable, but when McCluskey talked to the admiral in his sea cabin, Halsey was adamant.

"Wade begged the admiral to let us go," Gray said later, "but the admiral said, 'No.' He said, 'The Army Air Corps is the defense of Hawaii. These fighters are here to defend this fleet.'"

Halsey's decision was not popular with his gung-ho young fighter pilots but it was a wise one. Had they entered the fight over Oahu, they would have tipped off the Japanese that an American carrier was in the vicinity. The carriers were the enemy's primary targets and they surely would have detached enough planes to go after it in force.

Had it been lost or even severely damaged, as probably would have happened given the Japanese numerical superiority at the moment, the fleet would have lost its ability to strike back as early as it did eight weeks later on February 1 when planes from the *Enterprise* and the newly-arrived carrier *Yorktown* attacked the Marshall and Gilbert Islands.

Instead, Fighting Six maintained its combat air patrol over the task force until sunset, even though it was fired on in error by its own anti-aircraft late that afternoon according to the Squadron diary.

Meanwhile, assorted destroyers and cruisers which had escaped damage in the attack, left Pearl Harbor to join the *Enterprise* task force. A message from Kimmel put Halsey in command of all the U.S. ships at sea in the area and he ordered them to rendezvous Monday about 150 miles west of Kauai at the northwestern end of the main islands in the Hawaiian chain.

That would include the *Lexington* task force which was only about 400 miles southeast of Midway when the Japanese struck Oahu. She was close to the point where she would launch the new fighters toward Midway and the planes were on the flight deck getting ready to take off. Instead, they were returned to the hangar deck and the task force reversed course.

Meanwhile, as evening approached, Pearl Harbor relayed to the *Enterprise* a report that an enemy naval force had been sighted south of Oahu. She launched torpedo planes and six fighters from Fighting Six but the "enemy" turned out to be American destroyers and cruisers from Pearl. The torpedo planes were ordered to return to the carrier but the fighters under Lieutenant Fritz Hebel were running low on gas.

"This group was directed to return to Ford Island at 2000 [8 p.m.]," the Fighting Six war diary recorded. "In accordance with instructions from Ford Island field tower, these planes proceeded at 1,000 feet with wheels down and running lights illuminated at 2110 [9:10 p.m.].

"At this time, all antiaircraft batteries of the U.S. fleet opened up on these planes. Jim Daniels and Gale Hermann landed at Ford Island immediately with numerous bullet holes in their planes. Hermann's ship had 18 holes in it. Eric Allen parachuted after having had his plane shot up."

Allen landed in the water alongside the battleship *California* which was resting in the mud under Battleship Row. He was wounded but got out of the water and was taken to the Naval dispensary where he died the next day.

Hebel's plane crashed and burned in a nearby sugarcane field where he was rescued and taken to Tripler Army hospital. He also died the next day. Ensign Herb Menges was killed instantly when his plane crashed and burned at Pearl City, just west of the harbor.

Daniels survived his first attempt to land by shining his landing lights directly at the gunners on Ford Island, blinding them long enough to permit him to escape. He swung left and dove for Barber's Point with his lights out, then made a low, fast approach to Ford Island again, landing with only one bullet hole in his plane.

Ensign Dave Flynn also escaped the initial fusillade and flew back to sea. Upon returning to Ford Island for another try, his engine cut out at 1,000 feet over Barber's Point where he parachuted safely.

Sam Brown and the other seaplane scout pilots watched all this from a hangar on Ford Island. "It was quite dark, although the flames from the burning ships lit up the night quite well," Sam said. They watched in horror as the *Enterprise* fighter pilots came under fire and went down.

"Needless to say, we aviators were pretty disgusted with this," Brown said.

As the *Enterprise* task force maneuvered in the darkness of Sunday night, Halsey considered his options. In his book,

Halsey Says "No!"

Admiral Halsey's Story written with Lieutenant Commander J. Bryan III in 1947, he said:

"Suppose that the enemy was located, and suppose that I could intercept him: what then? A surface engagement was out of the question since I had nothing but cruisers to oppose his heavy ships. In addition, we were perilously low on fuel; the *Enterprise* was down to 50 percent of her capacity, the cruisers to 30 percent, the destroyers to 20 percent. On the other hand, my few remaining planes might inflict some damage and by the next afternoon the *Lexington's* task force would reach a position from which her air group could support an attack. If only someone would give us the straight word!"

The next morning, the *Big E* launched her Combat Air Patrol at dawn as usual and maintained it throughout the day. For the next eight days, with time out for a quick refueling visit to Pearl Monday night, she patrolled the area, mostly north of Oahu, the tedium relieved only by news that the *Lurline* reached San Francisco safely on December 10 with Peggy and Dougie Gray and the families of a number of others of the *Big E's* crew.

11: The Peace Envoys

As I drove into downtown Honolulu from Hickam, the city seemed to be strangely calm for having been through such a morning. There was little evidence of the Japanese attack in this part of town and the excitement which Mac had found earlier had dissipated.

However, away from the immediate downtown area, I was to learn later, there was considerable damage and a number of civilian dead and wounded, apparently caused by Japanese bombs.

I drove into the *Advertiser's* parking lot on the far side of downtown and hurried inside. As I passed the telephone switchboard just inside the big front doors, Betty, the pretty operator-receptionist, threw me a cheery hello. I noticed, however, that she wasn't wearing the flower which she usually had in her hair over one ear—evidence, perhaps, of the hurry with which she and the rest of the staff had reported to work.

The Peace Envoys

Curving flights of stairs rose to the right and left from the lobby to the second floor, providing a view of the lovely interior patio full of tropical trees and plants and open to the sky above. It made the *Advertiser* the most unusual and beautiful newspaper plant I'd ever seen.

When I entered our office on the second floor just off the *Advertiser* news room, Tyree was busy at the teletype transcribing incoming news from New York. Dick Richards' receiving station was in operation and copy from the rest of the world was flowing. Most of it was from Washington, D.C., including the White House announcement of the attack and Secretary of State Cordell Hull's bitter denunciation of the Japanese "peace envoys."

Ambassador Kichisaburo Nomura and Special Envoy Saburo Kurusu had been with Hull while the bombing was going on, although apparently none of them was aware of the attack at the time. On instructions from Tokyo, the Japanese had requested a meeting for 1 p.m., EST (7:30 a.m. Hawaiian time) and had been given an appointment for 1:45 p.m., just 20 minutes after the attack started. The meeting actually began at 2:20 p.m. (8:50 a.m., HST), about 10 minutes after the second wave of Japanese attackers swooped down on Oahu.

Nomura handed Hull Japan's reply to a U.S. document of November 26 which had set forth America's principles in the dispute over Japan's expansionism in the Far East. In stiff language, the Japanese paper rejected the U.S. position.

After reading the document with growing anger but still unaware of events in Hawaii, Hull fixed the Japanese with an icy glare and said:

"I must say that in all my conversations with you during the last nine months, I have never uttered one word of

51

untruth. This is borne out by the record. In all my 50 years of public service, I have never seen a document that was so crowded with infamous falsehoods and distortions on a scale so huge that I never imagined until today that any government on this planet was capable of uttering them."

As the two Japanese listened uncomfortably to Hull's indignant statement, the *Arizona* already had exploded with huge loss of life and was burning fiercely, the *Oklahoma* had capsized and most of the army, navy and Marine aircraft on Oahu had been destroyed or disabled. We had little more than anti-aircraft guns, machine guns and brave men to fight the second Japanese wave which was wreaking new havoc among the ships in the harbor and at Oahu's air bases.

It was immediately apparent that the Japanese had planned for months to strike without warning at the heart of the American military establishment in the Pacific while negotiations seemed to be continuing in good faith. Since the U.S. would not concede them a free hand, they had decided to achieve the goals of their East Asia Co-prosperity Sphere with military might after first disabling the only force they believed might be able to stop them.

Mac McCarthy came in a few minutes later and the three of us sat down to compare notes and make plans. Thank God Mac had been bumped off that plane to Manila. It was going to be bad enough with only three of us. If Bill and I had been alone, it might have been more than we could handle.

We had no idea how long the navy would keep commercial communications closed, whether it would be hours, days or weeks. Nor did we know what they would let us send when they did let us file again. None of us had ever worked under censorship nor covered a war. Our experience with the military was limited to Bill's and my contacts right there in Hawaii for the past year and a half.

Obviously, however, we had to be ready to file a complete, detailed story of what had happened as soon as communications reopened, supplemented by all the feature material we could gather—human interest stories, accounts of military and civilian heroics, how the Territory of Hawaii was coping with blackouts, rationing, military restrictions, etc., etc. The censors might not let it go, but we had to prepare it anyway.

First, we had to assemble verifiable facts, to find out what really had happened. All we knew for sure at that time was that there was heavy damage to warships and installations at Pearl Harbor and aircraft and buildings at Hickam.

We had heard about serious damage at Wheeler Field, the army's fighter plane base next to Schofield Barracks, the main infantry base, which also had been attacked. Apparently Kaneohe Naval Air Station on windward Oahu had been hit heavily and the Japanese also had struck the army's Bellows Field and the Marines' Ewa Field.

There were lots of reports of Japanese bombs in Honolulu and of dead and wounded civilians. By 10:30 a.m., the emergency hospital reported six dead and 21 wounded and Queens Hospital was calling for blood donors.

A bomb was reported to have fallen shortly before 9:30 a.m. near Governor Joseph Poindexter's residence, Washington Place, on the outskirts of downtown while he was conferring with Territorial Secretary Charles M. Hite

53

on preparation of an emergency proclamation. It killed a man across the street.

Another bomb was reported about 200 feet from Iolani (ee-oh-la-knee) Palace, seat of the Territorial Government, about 11:30 a.m. The Honolulu fire department answered nine calls within the first 90 minutes of the attack including the one from Hickam Field where they sent one engine company. Despite all this and the radio warnings, hundreds of Honoluluans drove to the top of Punchbowl, the extinct volcano behind the city, to watch the action.

Governor Poindexter declared a state of emergency for the entire territory at 10:05 a.m. under Hawaii's M-Day Law, passed only a few months earlier. It gave him almost dictatorial powers.

The army had ordered civilians off the streets and highways and appealed to them not to use their telephones. However, all army, navy and civil defense workers, except women, had been ordered to duty. But then, at 10:10 a.m., had come an order for civil defense workers not to report to Pearl Harbor. This apparently was dictated by the huge traffic jam which had built up on Dillingham Boulevard, the main road to Pearl, and it soon was rescinded. One thing the navy needed was the yard's workers.

As we talked, word came that a complete blackout had been ordered effective at sundown. No lights could be shown in any home or business building and all night time traffic was prohibited unless the headlights were off. Civilians weren't supposed to be on the streets anyway.

The Captain of the Port of Honolulu ordered all aids to navigation extinguished—buoys, channellights, and light-houses.

Residential water users were instructed to fill their bathtubs as a precaution against interruption of service and there were reports that the water might be contaminated. These were refuted the next day.

There were persistent reports that Japanese parachutists had landed at several different spots on Oahu. Mac picked up one report himself off an army teletype at Fort Shafter and related it in one of his reports to UP, but they all proved to be false.

Since we had to man the office overnight, not knowing what might happen, we had to plan a 24-hour schedule among the three of us, at least for the immediate future. We decided that Mac and I would stay at the office that night while Bill went home to be with Beth and their infant daughter, Sharon. He would return early Monday morning. As we sat there trying to sort fact from fiction, the phone rang. "Shay," said a sodden voice, "Whash goin' on around here, anyway?"

We knew a little more that he did, but not a lot.

12:   The Rumor Mill

As the afternoon wore on, we compiled reports from our own experiences, the *Advertiser* staff and the results of telephone checks around town. The military was saying nothing and the town was full of rumors ranging from the possible to the ridiculous. Among them, we noted these:

1. That five battleships had been sunk along Battleship Row at Pearl Harbor—the *Arizona, Oklahoma, West Virginia, Tennessee* and *Maryland*. In addition, the *Nevada*, although damaged, got under way and sought to escape. As she approached the harbor exit, more Japanese planes hit her causing further heavy damage. To prevent her from sinking there and blocking the exit, her crew ran her aground.

2. That about 40% of the fighter planes at Wheeler Field had been destroyed and that there was extensive damage to aircraft and buildings at Hickam Field and at the Naval Air Station on Ford Island.

3. That there had been attempts to block traffic headed

for Pearl Harbor on Dillingham Boulevard by overturning or stalling cars and trucks and that Marines at the Pearl Harbor gate had used machine guns to prevent such an effort there.

4. That Japanese parachutists had landed at a number of places on Oahu.

5. That Filipinos armed with cane knives had attacked civilian Japanese on the Big Island of Hawaii, seeking revenge.

6. That four Japanese troop transports were off Oahu.

7. That a Japanese aircraft carrier had been sunk.

8. That class rings from the University of Hawaii and Honolulu's McKinley High School had been found on the pilots of some of the few Japanese planes which had been shot down.

9. That mysterious fires had been sighted at several locations which either were signals to the attackers or the result of sabotage.

10. That Admiral Kimmel had been shot.

11. That a mysterious advertisement relating to Japanese silk in the Honolulu newspapers December 6 was a signal to local Japanese that the attack was coming.

12. That a Japanese who closed his soft drink stand at Pearl City landing on the west side of Pearl Harbor on December 6 after running it for some years really was a Japanese naval officer and spy.

13. That local Japanese using machetes had cut huge arrows in the cane fields Saturday night to direct Japanese fliers toward their targets Sunday morning.

14. That Honolulu's water supply had been poisoned or otherwise contaminated.

15. That Japanese amateur radio operators were caught

apparently communicating with enemy aircraft carriers and planes and that other Japanese were seized photographing damage to military objectives.

16. That the liner *Lurline* , which had left Honolulu Friday, had been sunk en route to San Francisco. This report even was heard on the *Enterprise* where it caused great concern for Jim Gray and others who had loved ones on the liner.

The first two reports about military damage smacked of the truth and, in fact, were very close to what actually had happened except that loss of aircraft was even greater than the rumors said. The others ranged from unlikely to illogical to ridiculous. None of them was true.

What was true was that the town—in fact, the whole Territory— was fighting mad. The anger was not confined to the military. Civilians were bitter and ready to fight.

"We'll get the little yellow bastards," was the common refrain. "Just wait 'til we get to Tokyo."

One of the best reports we got on the action in Pearl Harbor came from an eye-witness account the *Advertiser* obtained from Dick Cornelius, a civilian who had been in the navy yard. He, too, said five battleships had been sunk and another severely damaged.

"It was just about 8 o'clock when the first planes were sighted over Pearl Harbor," Cornelius said. "Previous to this, planes—with the Rising Sun plainly visible on their fuselages—had got Wheeler Field and Hickam Field. I didn't see a single one of our planes in the air.

"The first planes were real low. They swung over Pearl Harbor from the direction of Hickam about 100 feet in the air with torpedoes hanging from their undercarriages.

"Along with the torpedo attack, they used divebombers

coming from great heights, one after another, nine in each formation. There were about 100 planes in all.

"I picked up a machine gun bullet which had spattered on the ground several yards away. I think some children were hit at Hickam Field housing.

"I saw at least 10 direct hits on the battleship *Oklahoma* which turned over on her port side and sank within 20 minutes. The planes began attacking the remainder of the fleet. The *Tennessee, West Virginia, Arizona* and *California* were sunk and the *Maryland* damaged. The *Nevada* got underway and she's out at sea."

Except for his report on the *Nevada*, which was beached inside the harbor to prevent her from sinking, and the fact that the torpedo caused an explosion that blew the *Arizona's* bow off before the *Oklahoma* went over, Cornelius' account proved to be remarkably accurate.

Although the attackers concentrated on military targets, Honolulu did not escape unscathed. Bombs were reported all over town, many buildings were damaged and dead and wounded jammed the hospitals. By the late afternoon, there were nine civilian dead at Queens hospital and close to 50 more wounded, many of them American-Japanese.

In addition to the doctors working at Queens, Honolulu civilian physicians volunteered for duty at the army's Tripler General hospital across the street from Fort Shafter. The wounded poured in there from the military bases. As the hospitals began to fill, the radio stations appealed for blood donors.

By the next morning, the count of civilian dead had risen to 49 and there were a hundred or more injured.

Later investigation, however, showed that only one of the reported hits in civilian areas actually was a bomb. All the rest were our own anti-aircraft shells. Improperly fused, they failed to explode in the air, then plummeted to the ground where they often did explode.

In fact, the Japanese pilots were assigned to much more important targets in Pearl Harbor and at Oahu's military airfields and that's what they concentrated on.

There was only one confirmed report of a deliberate attack on a civilian target. At *Wahiawa* (wa-hee-a-wa), a village near Wheeler Field, a couple of Japanese planes sprayed the main street with machine gun fire before one of them crashed into a house and exploded in flames, killing the pilot.

Despite what was thought to be the bombing of the city, reports of huge damage to the fleet and the island's air defenses and rumors of all kinds, the populace did not panic that Sunday. Instead, they responded then and later with anger but also with discipline, general good will and a minimum of grumbling about the sudden changes in their lives wrought by the new circumstances.

In its three extras that day, the *Star-Bulletin* ran a brief editorial on the front page which set the tone for the days ahead:

"Honolulu and Hawaii will meet the emergency of war today as Honolulu and Hawaii have met emergencies in the past—cooly, calmly and with immediate and complete support of the officials, officers and troops who are in charge.

"Governor Poindexter and the army and navy leaders have called upon the public to remain calm; for civilians who have no essential business on the streets to stay off; and for every man and woman to do his duty.

"That request, coupled with the measures promptly

taken to meet the situation that has suddenly and terribly developed, will be heeded.

"Hawaii will do its part—as a loyal American territory.

"In this crisis, every difference of race, creed and color will be submerged in the one desire and determination to play the part that Americans always play in crisis."

I could see Editor Riley Allen's hand in that.

At 4 p.m. Governor Poindexter, who had talked with President Roosevelt by telephone about noon, declared martial law and even stronger action than his earlier declaration of an emergency under the M-Day law. Monday morning General Short took charge of the territorial government.

That Short and others believed that the Japanese attack was part of an invasion plan was indicated by his reference to it four times in his seven-paragraph proclamation which began:

"The military and naval forces of the Empire of Japan have attacked and attempted to invade these islands."

That invasion never was part of the meticulous Japanese plan may have been one of the biggest mistakes they ever made. Hawaii was their's for the taking that Sunday night.

13: That's a Bomb Shelter? (Kay)

With our egg-nog brunch behind us, we went back to the radio, listening to the news or as much as the announcers could tell us. Mostly we talked about our husbands. We were worried sick.

Mine, at least, was in town or somewhere nearby I was pretty sure, but the others had no idea what might be happening to their husbands or how their ships and friends may have fared. And none of us knew what might come next. Would the Japanese invade? Would they make another air attack? How bad was the damage? What lay ahead for all of us?

Sue Davidson was particularly upset because it was her wedding anniversary. "Bob and I were going to the Royal [Hawaiian hotel] for dinner and dancing tonight." she lamented. "We were really going to celebrate —champagne, the works."

Hidden in the minds of each of us, unspoken but very real, was fear—fear of the worst, fear that they might have been wounded or even killed. And if they got through

62

today, what then?   Even correspondents get killed, I thought.

We talked of our families on the mainland, too. Sue, Mary and I were from Pasadena in California and Anne was from South Pasadena. Ruth was from Houston. We knew our families would be terribly worried about us but there was no way we could let them know that we were all right, at least so far.

It never occurred to me that my family and Frank's, at least, would know that we were still alive because of our news reports. Frank's by-line was on the UP story from Honolulu and friends told me later they had heard me on the radio. Actually they had not because, in those days before tape recordings, my telephone conversation with Jim Sullivan had not been recorded. What they probably heard was a re-creation of the UP story of my report, a practice which was fairly common in radio broadcasting then. But, at least, our families knew we had survived the attack, even though I didn't know they knew.

From time to time we'd go outside across the footbridge to the driveway and the grassy terrace at the brow of the hill. The view there was extensive from Diamond Head on the left to Barbers Point beyond Pearl Harbor on the right.

Because the view was so good, quite a few of our neighbors along Alewa Drive came onto the estate to take advantage of it. Some brought with them some of the rumors that were circulating in the city such as the one about local Japanese cutting arrows in the cane fields to direct the Japanese planes to their targets.

At the time, such things did not seem to be too far-fetched. Given calmer consideration later on, we had to wonder how anyone, including ourselves, could have taken them seriously.

For one thing, it would have been a monumental task to cut such arrows by hand under the best conditions. To think of doing it at night in groups small enough to escape detection was preposterous. For another thing, the Japanese pilots had no need of assistance. Investigation in later years showed that the Japanese navy was very well informed about Pearl Harbor, ship locations and our airfields.

Some of the other rumors were easier to believe such as reports that Japanese paratroopers had landed in the hills behind us, that the water supply had been poisoned or that Japanese troop transports were offshore. I was glad I had thought to fill the bathtub with water.

All day, we watched the smoke pour up from Pearl Harbor although it diminished as the day wore on. Occasionally we heard the scream of what we thought was a falling bomb, then an explosion.

We didn't know it then but the Japanese had finished their work and would not return, fortunately for us.

In the afternoon we decided to take a look at our air raid shelter. Everyone in Honolulu had been told to dig a bomb shelter in his yard, and our neighbor in the main house on the estate, an army colonel named Whisner, the ROTC instructor at Punahou School, had had one dug for all of us about two months earlier.

I didn't know anything about military matters and certainly nothing about bomb shelters, but I didn't feel very confident about this one. It was located near the driveway, just over the brow of the hill facing Honolulu and the sea beyond. I guess it would have protected us from bomb or shell splinters but it didn't seem to me that it would have been much use against a stray bomb from an aerial attack or a shell from a navy bombardment of the city.

Anyway, this seemed to be the time to inspect it just in case we had to take refuge there. Gingerly I opened the entrance door which lay flat against the side of the hill. A couple of steps led down into the dark, dank interior.

Someone shined a flashlight into the shelter. There was a narrow bench along the back wall. Then the light revealed a myriad of creepy-crawly things. The place was filled with every kind of spider, centipede and other type of bug you could imagine, probably including a few poisonous scorpions. We probably should have lugged some food or a least a few containers of water up there but instead we just slammed the door on it and retreated. That was no place for us. Let the bombs fall. Better bombs than bugs as far as we were concerned.

Late in the afternoon Frank called from the bureau. Thank God he was safe. He said there had been a lot of damage to ships at Pearl Harbor, that several battleships had been sunk and that Hickam was a mess. Of course, he didn't know what was going to happen either. I told him that Anne and the other girls were with me and that Anne was going to spend the night. We hadn't heard from Sam.

Frank said he would have to stay at the office overnight but that he would try to get home for awhile in the morning. He reminded me that everything had to be blacked out at dusk. Suddenly, I realized that we had things to do.

14: Spies and Bugged Phones

When it became apparent that Oahu was under Japanese attack, Police Chief William A. Gabrielson assigned four policemen to guard the Japanese consulate on *Nuuanu* (noo-oo-ah-noo) Avenue, a few blocks from downtown. When they smelled smoke late in the morning, they called for help.

Seven detectives headed by Lieutenant Benjamin Van Kuren, chief of detectives and Lieutenant Yoshio Hasegawa, a Japanese-American, arrived at 12:20 p.m. They found Consul General Nagao Kita standing on the steps being interviewed by a reporter from the *Star-Bulletin*.

Ignoring Kita, the police rushed up the steps and forced their way into the main hallway. Here the smell of burning paper was strong, probably the reason that Kita had refused to let the reporter in.

Van Kuren and his men rushed down the hall, broke

into a rear room and surprised three consulate staff members around a fire burning in a washtub into which they were feeding consular reports and documents. The doors of several safes stood open. The detectives threw water on the fire and rescued as many of the papers as possible. They took Kita into custody and turned the papers over to the FBI.

Kita's interview with the Star-Bulletin reporter was his second that morning. Earlier, Kita refused to believe, or would not admit, that a Japanese attack was in progress. He said he thought all the explosions and firing had to do with "maneuvers" by U.S. forces.

The reporter went back to his office and returned with the *Star-Bulletin's* first extra which carried the huge headline, "WAR! OAHU BOMBED BY JAPANESE PLANES."

It was then that Kita and other members of his staff dashed for the code room and started the burning which Van Kuren and his men interrupted.

Meanwhile, Kita had returned to the reporter to finish the interview in which he urged all Japanese in the islands to "remain calm and law abiding."

It was no secret to army and navy intelligence, the FBI and the Honolulu police, that the consulate was the center of Japanese espionage in Hawaii. The fact that they knew that did not mean, however, that they could do anything about it.

Commercial communications facilities, which the consulate used extensively in making its reports to Tokyo, were protected under law, and the legal activities of the consulate staff were protected under the rules of diplomacy. There was nothing the intelligence agencies or police could do unless they caught a spy red-handed. This they never did.

For a long time, it was a simple matter for the consulate—or anyone else—to follow the comings and goings of the Pacific fleet. Since the navy was such an integral part of the Honolulu community, the movement of its ships in and out of Pearl Harbor naturally was of considerable general interest. Consequently, the Honolulu press reported them regularly, at least until the spring of 1941 when the navy requested that the practice stop.

But even then, it was not difficult for the casual observer to keep track of military activity around Oahu. Ship movements in and out of the navy base generally occurred during daylight hours and anyone living, or even driving, on the heights behind the city could keep track of them if he wanted to.

Other military movements weren't hard to discover either. One day, months before the Pearl Harbor attack, I got a tip that a squadron of navy patrol bombers had been transferred to the Philippines. With tension growing in the Pacific and before wartime censorship, any news that indicated a possible shift in the general situation was considered fair reporting.

It wasn't hard to check out the report. I simply talked with a few used car dealers, found one who recently had taken in a number of cars at one time, checked the names of the sellers and ascertained that they all were from that squadron.

About a week after I filed the story I had a visit from a young officer in the local Office of Naval Intelligence, curious about the source of my story which he admitted was accurate. Of course I did not tell him but I assured him it was not from anyone connected with the navy.

That story wasn't very important, and I don't believe it tipped the balance of power in the Pacific nor endangered any lives, but it earned me more attention from Naval Intelligence than I wanted or deserved. Whether it resulted from that or something else, I never new, but not long after the war started I became suspicious that my home phone was being tapped.

In 1949, when I was the Los Angeles bureau manager, I was on a Pan American Inaugural flight to introduce a new long-range airplane to the transPacific service to Tokyo. We picked up a group of businessman and news people in Honolulu en route including Robert E. Shivers who had been the FBI chief in Hawaii before and during the war. Now he was in private business.

We had a midnight departure from Honolulu so most of us went to sleep as soon as we were air-borne. As I dozed in my seat a few hours later, I became aware of someone standing in the aisle looking down at me. It was Bob.

"Did you ever know who it was who was bugging your phone in Honolulu?" he asked.

"Well, I always assumed it was Waldo," I said, referring to Commander (later Rear Admiral) Waldo Drake, Fleet Public Information Officer. "Nope," Bob said. "It was Captain Mayfield." Mayfield was the 14th Naval District (Hawaii) Intelligence chief and it was one of his staffers who had questioned me about the patrol squadron story.

As pre-war tension in the Pacific worsened in 1941, the navy tried hard to keep a lid on all information about ship movements. This included strict instructions to navy dependents to keep their mouths shut. A gossipy navy wife faced the probability of being shipped home to the States if she were caught discussing her husband's whereabouts and it could earn him a black mark on his fitness report too.

Anne Brown ran into that problem one day in 1941. She and Janet Hahn, wife of one of Sam's shipmates, had gone to the officers club liquor store at the Submarine Base to replenish their household supply. While they were there, the New Orleans returned to port, quite unexpectedly as far as the girls were concerned. Anne and Janet were thoroughly surprised when their husbands walked into the O Club but an observer thought otherwise.

"We did not know," Anne said, "but we had a hard time convincing the powers that be that we were okay."

Japanese servants and shop keepers also were suspect, at least among those who saw a spy behind every Japanese face. Dinner party and cocktail talk frequently dwelled on these suspicions since many officers and their families lived off base in the civilian community.

Among the favorite spy stories were those dealing with servants and with trades people, particularly food vendors. Pete Willett tells the story of a Japanese who ran a grocery store in Pearl City, a small community just west of Pearl Harbor.

"I think his name was Asada or something like that," Pete said. "He had one of those trucks where the fruit and vegetables are displayed and he would come by every morning about 10 o'clock. Not only could you buy whatever vegetables you needed, you also could order any meat you wanted which he would deliver the next day, or even that afternoon, if necessary. Often, that was better than going to the commissary. He knew everyone and I guess he was an excellent grocer.

"It was the norm for a wife to say things like, 'I'm going to need a good rib roast this coming Friday for about 20 people. The *Yorktown* (or whatever) is coming in.' If anyone knew the comings and goings of the navy, it was Mr. Asada. We later heard that he was a lieutenant commander in the Japanese navy and had been set up in business something like 12 years earlier. He allegedly was the source of the mooring maps the Japanese carried."

While such stories made good conversation, and perhaps some of them even had some smattering of truth about them, it's doubtful that the Japanese consulate needed or depended on such help. The consulate had its own master spy.

15: Scotch and Sake

The consulate's master spy had been on its staff since Spring. In *At Dawn We Slept*, Gordon Prange discusses Japanese espionage in Hawaii in considerable detail, especially the work of Takeo Yoshikawa, the Japanese Navy's top spy who joined the consulate later in March under an alias, Tadashi Morimura.

He spent the rest of the year, according to Prange, gathering precise and detailed information about the patterns of ship movements in and out of Pearl Harbor, their normal mooring locations and the defenses of Oahu.

This he did by careful observation on frequent trips through the countryside in the Pearl Harbor area. Sometimes he went in a taxi driven by a local Japanese, John Mikani, who frequently worked for the consulate, sometimes in a car borrowed from another consular staffer.

He found a number of locations with good views of the

naval base and Hickam Field, including—unbeknownst to us, of course—a two story teahouse on Alewa Heights not far up the road from our home.

He kept meticulous records noting patterns of timing for movements of elements of the fleet and flights of patrol planes, and he apparently was the principle source of the information on which the Japanese based their plan of attack.(3)

A note in my diary dated December 8, 1941 in a section recapping what we knew then about the attack and events leading up to it said, "The FBI apparently was all set to take [Japanese] leaders into custody when the attack broke. However, it appears that the FBI and intelligence services were unable to cope with spy activities earlier.

"In this connection, it seems noteworthy that the *Taiyo Maru,* which brought American-Japanese back to Hawaii November 1, laid over for five days for no apparent reason and departed November 5, arriving in Tokyo November 15. Charts and instructions found on (downed) Japanese airmen were dated November 16. . . ."

Prange, whose research of the events leading up to the attack on Pearl Harbor was extraordinary, provides considerable detail on how Kita and his staff delivered extensive reports from Yoshikawa to Japanese intelligence agents on the *Taiyo Maru.*(4)

Primary Japanese targets in Pearl Harbor were aircraft carriers and battleships and the charts carried by Japanese pilots were quite accurate in showing where they normally berthed. My diary noted that the tanker *Ogalala,* which was sunk, was in a berth occupied by the battleship *Pennsylvania* the day before when she moved to a drydock across the channel. The target ship *Utah,* also sunk, moved into the *Lexington's* berth when the carrier went to sea December 5.

Of course Yoshikawa, ostensibly a minor member of the consular staff, was unknown to me and to almost anyone else in Honolulu. Consul General Kita, however, was quite well know in the city both among the American-Japanese and the *haoles* (haow-lees), or caucasians. His vice consul, Otojiro Okuda, having served as acting consul general before Kita's arrival only a few weeks before Yoshikawa's, also was quite well known in the community.

My acquaintance with them was brief but interesting. In early November, negotiations between Secretary of State Cordell Hull and the Japanese ambassador, Admiral Kichisaburo Nomura, were close to stalemate. Nomura, a career navy officer called out of retirement a year earlier to become ambassador to the United States, needed help. He suggested that the Foreign Office send a veteran diplomat to Washington to support him.

Tokyo responded by naming Ambassador Saburo Kurusu to be a special envoy to join the talks. Kurusu, an experienced diplomat with an American wife and a good command of English, caught Pan American's *China Clipper* in Hong Kong on November 7 and headed for Washington.

The plane was scheduled to arrive in Honolulu on November 10 and I planned to meet it and attend the press conference he probably would hold since Honolulu would be the first stop on his journey at which time American press would see him. I also wanted something more extensive than that however—an exclusive interview if possible.

It happened that John Morris, UP's Asia division manager, was in Honolulu for a few days en route to the mainland on vacation so I enlisted John's help. He had met Kurusu and was well acquainted with Kita whom he had known when they both were stationed in China. John called him and he invited us to come to the consulate to meet Kurusu during his Honolulu layover.

However, the *Clipper* was delayed by engine trouble for two days at Midway Island. My dispatch on November 9 reporting the delay noted with some irony that passengers on the *Clipper* with Kurusu included eight American pilots en route home after ferrying American war planes to reinforce Singapore against the Japanese threat. Another passenger was William Keswick, a British Far Eastern expert who had been shot and wounded the previous year by a Japanese member of the Shanghai Municipal Council of which Keswick was chairman.

When Kurusu finally reached Honolulu at 4:45 p.m. November 12, my first bulletin said he was "smilingly reticent" to discuss his mission with Honolulu newspeople.

Part of his reticence may have been caused by the hub-bub which greeted him in the Pan American terminal. In those days it was only a small, one-story wooden building, not nearly as well appointed as a terminal one might find today at the smallest municipal airport. Consequently, the tiny waiting room was noisy and crowded with passengers and with Japanese Americans on hand to greet the special envoy.

There seemed to be no place for him to talk to the small press contingent. Finally, however, he agreed to meet us, all males except for Lynne Croft of the *Star-Bulletin*, in the relatively congenial atmosphere of the ladies' lounge. It was the only quiet space available.

He was not much more forthcoming there, stating simply that he was on "a very difficult and important mission," that it was "the common responsibility of the United States and Japan to maintain peace in the Pacific and that he was hopeful that this could be done."

75

As we left the ladies' room, Kita pulled John aside and said Kurusu would not be able to meet us for an exclusive interview, after all, because the long delay at Midway had left him so little time in Honolulu, time he needed for meetings with leaders of the Japanese-American community. Perhaps by way of apology, Kita said he and Okuda would like us to be their guests for dinner at a Japanese teahouse two nights later. We accepted.

There were many Japanese teahouses in the Islands ranging from modest little mom-and-pop establishments to quite elaborate ones. They were frequented by the Japanese population, of course, and often by *haoles* as well. The teahouse in which we met Kita and Okuda was one of the more elegant. It was located on Nuuanu Avenue, not far from the consulate, and was one of the best known in Honolulu.

I parked on Nuuanu and John and I walked down a narrow concrete walk alongside a two-story wooden house. When we reached the back of the house, we entered a lovely garden full of flowers and tropical plants. Around three sides of the perimeter were a number of private dining rooms looking out on the garden when their parchment-covered sliding doors were open, but private when the doors were closed.

A Japanese lady in the traditional brocaded kimono and wide bright sash, called *obi* (oh-bee), met us with smiles and bows and conducted us to one of the private rooms. She presented each of us with a pair of Japanese slippers.

"Please," she said, motioning us to sit on the top of two steps leading into the building. We took off our shoes, donned the slippers and she ushered us inside, sliding the door closed behind us.

We entered a typical Japanese room—thick, cushiony

wall-to-wall straw mat on the floor and nearly bare of furniture except for a couple of very low tables. There were Japanese paintings on the fixed walls and a sliding parchment partition divided our room from the next, apparently a serving room.

Kita and Okuda awaited us, each wearing a handsome kimono. A woman servant handed each of us a plain kimono to replace the suit jackets in which we had arrived. Kita invited us to sit, which meant getting down on the floor since this was strictly Japanese style—no chairs, only cushions to support us as we pushed our legs under a low table.

A gracious servant, also in kimono and obi and with her jet-black hair done in the traditional Japanese style, adjusted cushions for us and handed us steaming hot, damp wash cloths with which to wipe our faces and hands.

I recall Kita as a rather short, blocky man, stockier than the average Japanese. He had a flat pug nose on a rather broad face which was all smiles this evening. Prange describes Okuda as alert and suave with strong features. I recall him as a slender, black-haired man, slightly taller than Kita but, rather than being suave, Okuda seemed to me to be slightly ill at ease, at least at the start of the evening.

Despite the setting, the evening was not to be entirely Japanese. The service lady quickly brought a bottle of scotch and four glasses, poured for each of us and disappeared. I suppose the scotch was for our benefit but I'm not a scotch drinker, particularly when it's served straight and warm. Nevertheless, I sipped mine politely.

After some conversation, Kita caught John's eye and raised his glass. *Kampai*, he said, giving John the Japanese equivalent of "bottoms up."

Kampai, John replied, raising his glass in return. They both drained the drinks.

Almost immediately, Okuda caught my eye and repeated the process. *Kampai,* I responded, and down went the scotch.

Okuda reached out and refilled the glasses. Again, after a little more conversation, *kampai,* said Kita, catching my eye this time. *Kampai,* said Okuda to John. Down went the scotch again.

Again the refills and again the *kampais* except that courtesy required that John and I take the initiative on the next two rounds. Another round and I began trying to look anywhere in the room but at our hosts. Fortunately, before much longer, the service lady reappeared with three assistants and the first course of a delicious meal.

Our table was just high enough off the floor to accommodate my folded knees as I sat on my cushion. The ladies knelt on the floor, one beside each of us to serve and, in my case, with much giggling, to help me handle the ivory chopsticks. Kita and Okuda were experts, of course, and John was very adept, having spent many years in the Orient, but I had not yet mastered the art. Plucking a few kernels of rice from a bowl or properly gripping a slippery vegetable or piece of raw fish long enough to get it to my mouth before it dropped on my clothes or the floor, was beyond my limited talent.

Warm *sake,* Japanese rice wine, accompanied the meal, of course, and the *kampais* continued. Fortunately, the thimble-sized cups in which warm sake is served hold only a small amount, but enough drops of water will wear away a stone and we were having enough *sake,* on top of the scotch, to wear away our brains. More *sake* went down when we played the traditional teahouse or *geisha* (gay-sha) house game of "scissors cut paper, rock breaks scissors, paper covers rock."

Scotch and Sake

Finally the meal and the games were over, but not the evening. John and I knew it was time to go, but Kita and Okuda insisted on more. The *kampais* continued until finally Okuda's head nodded. He gently slid from a sitting to a prone position. Then Kita collapsed nearby.

John and I crawled quietly to the door, remembering to retrieve our jackets as we went. We crawled outside on hands and knees, slipped out of our slippers and into our shoes, then carefully rose to our feet.

The garden was quiet and no noise came from the other rooms. With our arms around each other's waists for support, we carefully made our way along the narrow walk to my car parked on Nuuanu. There were no designated drivers in those days. Had there been, neither of us would have qualified, but we made it home safely.

I've always wondered whether the consul general and his deputy were just over-enthusiastic hosts or whether they thought they could learn something useful from a couple of indiscreet reporters. If so, they must have been disappointed as well as hung over. They surely knew a lot more about the United States fleet and the defenses of Hawaii than we did!

16: In the Black Hell-hole

The battleship *Oklahoma* took one of the first hits from the Japanese torpedo bombers. She lay outboard of the *Maryland* at the south end of Battleship Row, exposed to the low-flying attackers.

There were two torpedo hits in rapid succession, then two more. Seaman J.F. Carroll was in his compartment below deck.

"We had no idea what was happening," he wrote two weeks later. "I rushed to my general quarters station (in the boiler control room) and was told the Japs were attacking.

"The ship began to list. Someone said it was going to turn over, but we did not believe she would. Then two more torpedoes hit us and the boiler control room was filled with smoke. Then word was passed that gas was in the ship and we were ordered to get out our gas masks.

"On arriving on the second deck, I saw lockers torn loose and sliding around the deck. Mess tables and bunks also were on the move and causing a great deal of injury to the personnel."

The third and fourth torpedo hits finished the *Oklahoma*. Slowly she began to roll over, then came to rest on her side, her bottom exposed obscenely.

"By the time we got our gas masks out of storage, word was passed to abandon ship." Carroll continued. "We had no lights and the public address system was out of commission.

"Men were getting out in every possible way. They were lined up at ports and hatches, all trying to make an opening for escape. I found a port where no one was near and made a rush for it. Fortunately there was a dog-wrench nearby. By the time I got the port open, the ship was lying on her side.

"I got out through the port and was standing on the side of the ship when an explosion from the *Arizona* knocked me down."

As Carroll picked himself up, scores of others were scrambling off the stricken ship's decks and down the side of the slanted hull.

"Just as I was about to leave for the water, I heard a call and it was the chaplain who was trying to get through the port where I had escaped," Carroll went on.

"I tried to pull him through. I got him as far through as the hips but could not pull him through entirely. Another sailor on the side of the ship gave me a hand, but we could not get him through. He told us to push him back so that others whom he was holding up could get out."[5]

The chaplain was not the only one who failed to get out of the ship. At least 32 did not make it and were trapped inside.

About 11 a.m., while ships blazed along Battleship Row and jittery gunners awaited another attack, a navy launch passed near the *Oklahoma*.

"Tap, tap, tap." It was a metallic sound like a hammer striking solid metal. "Tap, tap, tap," it came again. The launch raced back to its dock for help and a crew of civilian navy yard workers rushed to the ship.

They scrambled up the sloping hull with cutting equipment, hugging the *Oklahoma's* side to avoid splinters from nearby explosions and anti-aircraft shells bursting in the air. They listened, then went to work.

They started cutting with acetylene torches but someone warned that there might be explosive or flammable fumes inside the hull, so they substituted slower but safer pneumatic cutting equipment. As night fell, they worked by the light of the fires on the blazing *Arizona* at the other end of Battleship Row.

It was hours before the workmen cut through the thick steel hull. Julio de Castro, a civilian navy yard worker, was in charge. "For about an hour, there was anti-aircraft fire all over the place," he said, "but we kept on working. When the firing got too hot, we'd flatten out against the hull and hope nothing would hit us." The men worked for hours. Finally, the first success. "We cut a small hole through a manhole hatch," de Castro said. "I reached through and pulled the dogs on the hatch and opened the manhole.

"The compartment was empty. But we knew that on the other side of it were men who had been tapping. I found another hatch. We went over there and shouted. Somebody shouted back. Boy, did that sound good! Those sailors were in there shouting like hell.

"Are you all right? I called. 'Yeah, we're all right so far,' someone shouted back. 'But the water's coming up faster. It's up to our waists now.'

"They kept shouting, 'For God's sake, hurry.' I told them to keep steady and listen to what I was telling them. 'Now

82

just one of you, one who is strong and well, do all the talking,' I said. 'The rest of you just keep quiet and keep your heads.' Say, those sailors were swell. It was early Monday morning now. Those sailors had been in the black space without light or anything else since early Sunday, but, by golly, they just quieted down and took my instructions.

"I told them to undog the hatch on their side because there was too much pressure on our side. We were using the pressure to keep the water down. Well, those six boys in there got the dogs off the hatch. It was about 6 o'clock Monday morning. They came piling out of there, naked as the day they were born. They knocked me down and I floundered in the water, but I didn't care. I didn't blame them for wanting to get out of that black hell hole."

Those were the first six of the 32 men rescued from inside the *Oklahoma*. De Castro's men continued to work until 7 p.m. Monday when they finally were relieved by another crew.

Working in noxious and possibly explosive fumes and with water rising slowly but steadily, the new men cut through a series of bulkheads to rescue five groups of trapped seamen, some of them waiting in water up to their armpits.

The relief crew brought out the last two men about 1 a.m. Tuesday, almost 38 hours after the rescue operation began.

De Castro and his exhausted men got back to their shop Monday evening a little after 7 p.m. after they had been relieved, eager to clean up and go home.

"Somebody came up to me while I was changing my clothes," de Castro said. "I was all in a hurry and wanted to get home. This guy asks me:

'Why didn't you fill out this overtime slip?'

I looks at him and says:

83

'*Christamighty.*'"!
Then de Castro walked five miles home through the blackout.(6)

17: "Let's Borrow a Boat"

Just before night fell on Ford Island Sunday, a messenger arrived at the hangar where Sam Brown and his scout plane pilots waited. Sam was summoned to a meeting in the office of Rear Admiral Patrick N.L. Bellinger, commander of the fleet's patrol wings.

"I went there and found a number of other aviators, mostly from the battleships," Sam said. "We discussed what could be done. It turned out that my four seaplane scouts and maybe five or six other small seaplanes were the only flyable navy aircraft available. All the others had been damaged or destroyed.

"It was decided to send out four of our seaplanes at dawn to search for the Japanese carriers. Just what we were supposed to do if we found them wasn't explained. I had a pretty firm idea that it would be a one-way trip if we did find them."

Sam returned to the hangar to find Mickey Reeves

anxiously awaiting his arrival. Mickey had a proposition for his friend. They would "borrow" a boat from the nearby boat shed, take it to the officers club dock near the submarine base where Sam's car was parked, and drive into Honolulu to see Ronney, Mickey's wife, whom he hadn't seen in 10 days.

"After some hesitation," said Sam, "I agreed to try it so the two of us worked our way down to the boat shed. Mind you, there were bomb holes and damaged buildings all along the way and even with the flames, everything was quite dark.

"When we arrived at the boat shed, we found it totally black inside. However, Mickey, by using his cigarette lighter, worked his way out onto a slip and found a whaleboat with the keys in the dash. We got the vessel started and proceeded to the officer's club landing.

The two felt their way through the dark up the ramp from the landing and into the parking lot where they found Sam's car undamaged.

"Unbeknownst to us," Sam continued, "the base Marines had posted Marines behind the bushes about every 100 yards along the road. As we proceeded, these men would jump out from behind the bushes, wave their rifles at us and yell, 'Douse those lights! Don't you know there's a war on? We've got a strict blackout.'

"Well, without our lights, it was so dark I couldn't see where to drive. After about three of these episodes with the gun-waving Marines, I stopped the car and asked the last one what we could do, explaining Mickey's anxiety about his wife."

The Marine told them that if they could get to Building 30 in the navy yard, there was a man there who could black out their lights. So, with Mickey walking ahead and Sam following in the car, they finally reached Building 30.

"After waiting for several cars ahead of us," Sam said, "we found a grizzled Marine sergeant with hash marks up to his elbow who would spray the front of our car, including the headlights, green! This, he said, would qualify our lights as blacked out. This for 50 cents!

"I said to Mickey, 'We're never going to lose this war with men like this on our side.'"

The greened-out lights were not enough, however. On the highway to Honolulu, jittery National Guardsmen kept jumping into the road, pointing their guns.

"That was just too dangerous and I finally said to hell with it," Sam said. "We turned around and drove back to the O-Club, took our boat back to the boat shed, walked back to the hangar and went to bed on some cots there."

But that wasn't the end of Sam's problems. More came with the dawn take-off for the four seaplane scouts.

"The damaged battleships had mounted machine guns along their sides to help repel any new Japanese attack," Sam said, "and they tried to shoot us down as we took off from the water next to Battleship Row. What a mess! "

The scout planes, despite the battleship's machine guns and the holes in their fabric from Sunday's flying debris, got off the water safely, but their attempt to find the Japanese attack force was futile. By that time, it was far beyond their limited range on its way back to Japan.

When the scouts reached the limit of their 200-mile search radius, they headed back toward Oahu. As they approached the island, their supply of gasoline rapidly diminishing, they were required to give a recognition signal so the island's defense forces would not attack them.

"They had told us that the recognition signal upon our

return was to circumnavigate Oahu (about 100 miles) before landing," Sam said. "This was a long trip for an SOC after a 200-mile search, and one of the boys ran out of gas and landed in the surf off Barber's Point and was lost. That was particularly dumb since there were no fighters to send up to intercept us even if we didn't have the recognition signal."

Waikiki Beach and the Royal Hawaiian Hotel
were popular with service men on leave

The Royal Hawaiian Hotel on Waikiki Beach was a rendezvous for both the military and civiliians.

Heading for the Royal Hawaiian Hotel. L to R Kay Tremaine, Frank Tremaine, Anne Brown, B.J. Thurston, Marie O'Hara.

Beach picnic at Bellows Field, Oahu, April 1941. L to R Lt. Sam Brown, Jr., Sue Davidson, Lt. (jg) Bob Davidson, Frank Tremaine, Kay Tremaine.

The 16" coast defense gun at Fort Weaver, near Pearl Harbor, was for protection against surface invasion.

Lt. General Walter C. Short commander of the Army's Hawaiian Department on Department 7, 1941.

Admiral Husband E. Kimmel, Commander-in-Chief Pacific Fleet in 1941, with his principal staff officers, Captain W.S. DeLany (L) and Captain W.W. Smith.

Special Envoy Saburo Kurusu assisted Ambassador Kichisaburo Nomura in negotiations in Washington before Pearl Harbor. His wife was American.

Japanese Ambassador Nomura and Special Envoy Kurusu leave the White House in Washington after failure of proposals several weeks before the Hawaii attack.

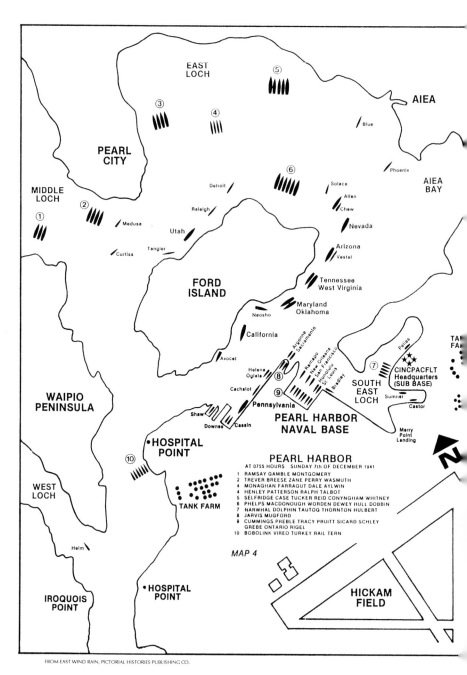

EAST
LOCH

⑤

AIEA

③

④

Blue

PEARL
CITY

⑥

Phoenix

AIEA
BAY

Detroit

Solace

MIDDLE
LOCH

Allen

②

Chew

Raleigh

Nevada

①

Medusa

Utah

Curtiss

Tangier

Arizona

Vestal

FORD
ISLAND

Tennessee
West Virginia

Neosho

Maryland
Oklahoma

California

Argonne
Sacramento

Avocet

Ramapo
New Orleans
San Francisco
Honolulu
St. Louis

Pelias

Helena
Oglala

⑧

CINCPACFLT
Headquarters
(SUB BASE)

⑦

WAIPIO
PENINSULA

Cachalot

⑨

Bradley

SOUTH
EAST
LOCH

Sumner

Castor

Pennsylvania

Shaw

PEARL HARBOR
NAVAL BASE

Downes   Cassin

Merry
Point
Landing

●HOSPITAL
POINT

⑩

TANK FARM

WEST
LOCH

PEARL HARBOR
AT 0755 HOURS   SUNDAY 7th OF DECEMBER 1941
1   RAMSAY GAMBLE MONTGOMERY
2   TREVER BREESE ZANE PERRY WASMUTH
3   MONAGHAN FARRAGUT DALE AYLWIN
4   HENLEY PATTERSON RALPH TALBOT
5   SELFRIDGE CASE TUCKER REID CONYNGHAM WHITNEY
6   PHELPS MACDONOUGH WORDEN DEWEY HULL DOBBIN
7   NARWHAL DOLPHIN TAUTOG THORNTON HULBERT
8   JARVIS MUGFORD
9   CUMMINGS PREBLE TRACY PRUITT SICARD SCHLEY
     GREBE ONTARIO RIGEL
10 BOBOLINK VIREO TURKEY RAIL TERN

Helm

MAP 4

HICKAM
FIELD

IROQUOIS
POINT

●HOSPITAL
POINT

FROM EAST WIND RAIN, PICTORIAL HISTORIES PUBLISHING CO.

Ship locations at Pearl Harbor on December 7, 1941.

Pearl Harbor from the southeast in October 1941. Ford Island in center, oil storage and submarine base, left center. Battleship Row at left of Ford Island.

Failing to strike the submarine base and oil storage tanks at Pearl Harbor was a major Japanese mistake.

The USS Ward (DD-139) fired the first U.S. shots in the
Pacific War, striking a Japanese midget submarine near the
entrance to Pearl Harbor.

This electrifying radio message alerted naval stations around
the world.

PBNY 3-7-41 35M **Original**	U.(NAVAL AIR STATION, KODIAK ALASK NAVAL COMMUNICATIONS	
Heading	NPC NR 63 F L Z F5L 071830 C8⸗ TARI 0 31	
From:	CINCPAC	Date 7 I
To:	ALL SHIPS PRESENT AT HAWAIIN AREA.	
Info:	– URGENT –	
DEFERRED unless otherwise checked	ROUTINE.......... PRIORITY..........	AIRMAIL

AIRRAID ON REARLHARBOR X THIS IS NO DRILL

A Japanese plane rises over Battleship Row and Ford Island as the attack begins, taken from another Japanese aircraft.

Tracks and shockwaves from Japanese torpedoes striking battleships, from a captured Japanese photograph. From left, Nevada; Vestal and Arizona; West Virginia; Tennessee.

Fuel oil spreads outward from the Oklahoma *(R) and* West Virginia. *Inboard from the right,* Maryland, Tennessee *and* Arizona, *whose magazine has not yet exploded.*

This Japanese aerial photograph shows ships burning in Battleship Row.

Smoke rises from the ships burning at Pearl Harbor, seen from Aiea Heights.

Fighter planes parked in rows at the Army Air Force's Wheeler Field made them easy targets for strafing.

Army P-40's were destroyed at Bellows Field.

America's first air aces in World War II were second lieutenants Ken Taylor (L) and George Welch flying P-40's from Haleiwa airstrip.

Gunners hastily assembled to repel invaders or enemy planes.

Pearl Harbor's main gate became a bottleneck on December 7.

The USS West Virginia *sank with a loss of 105 men.*

Sailors in a motor launch approach the burning West Virginia *seeking anti-aircraft ammunition.*

Sailors begin a cleanup of Ford Island Naval Air Station while ships burn in the distance.

Thirty-three of the 36 PBY Catalina patrol planes at Kaneohe Naval Air Station were damaged or destroyed in the attack.

Capsized battleship Oklahoma *with USS* Maryland *behind, lost 415 men. The visible hole is probably the one through which 32 sailors were rescued.*

Minelayer USS Oglala *rolled over and sank after being moved from alongside cruiser USS* Helena *at left at 1010 (Ten-ten) Dock.*

Destroyers Cassin *and* Downes, *beyond repair, were scrapped. Battleship* Pennsylvania, *in the background of Drydock One, was only slightly damaged.*

Navy Yard drydocks following the attack. Cassin, Downes *and* Pennsylvania *are in Drydock One at the bottom; bowless destroyer* Shaw *at center top.*

The Honolulu Star Bulletin *printed three extras after presses of the rival Honolulu* Advertiser *broke down.*

Most of the damage to homes and stores in Honolulu was caused by shells fired from American ships in Pearl Harbor.

Several civilians were killed when a projectile exploded near their car.

Wing of Japanese Nakajima Kate torpedo bomber, one of five shot down.

Nakajima torpedo bomber after souvenir hunters removed Rising Sun.

Message and drawing found in a downed Japanese plane.

This B-17 bomber, destroyed at Bellows Field, was probably one arriving from California as the Japanese attack was beginning.

Ensign Sakamaki, sole survivor of the five midget submarines released at Pearl Harbor, was not included in this painting; he was in disgrace for surviving.

The controls of Sakamaki's submarine. A faulty compass, at the right of the wheel, apparently caused him to go astray, miss Pearl Harbor.

Admiral Chester Nimitz was promoted by President Roosevelt over 28 admirals senior to him.

Admiral Nimitz assumed command of the Pacific Fleet on 31 December 1941 on board the submarine Grayling at Pearl Harbor.

Fleet Admiral Nimitz signs the Instrument of Surrender on USS Missouri, ending World War Two.

18: Not There --Dust Balls (Kay)

Suddenly the blackout was our principal concern. The instructions we had heard on the radio were explicit. There was to be a complete blackout. Not a light could show, not even a pinpoint.

Our little house was not built for blackouts. There was a curtain on the one window in the bathroom and translucent shades on the two windows in the bedroom, but that was it. There were no curtains, shades or blinds for the long windows in the living room-dining area which looked toward the sea in three directions. The kitchen window, looking toward Pearl Harbor, had nothing over it either.

The stove burned gas, producing a blue flame when lit, of course. How that little bit of light could be seen at any distance through the kitchen window, which was higher than the level of the stove top, was beyond me. Nevertheless, the instructions were definite—not even that much light could show.

89

Dusk was approaching and night falls rapidly in Hawaii. There is no twilight so we had to get moving. The quickest thing to cook that I had available was veal chops, so we threw those on the stove. Somebody made a tossed green salad and we sat down to a quick meal at the table in the dining ell.

By now, it was almost dark outside and even darker inside. Off in the distance to the west we could see the glow of fires still burning at Pearl Harbor. It was a gloomy meal.

When we finished it was far too dark to try to do the dishes so we just left them for morning.

Sue and Anne were smokers and liked a cigarette after dinner but that was out, too. You wouldn't dare light a match or lighter anywhere it might be seen and the radio announcements had warned against letting even the glow of a cigarette show.

We sat there in the living room for awhile, not talking much. We'd talked too much already about all the horrible possibilities. There was no point in going over that ground again. We all faced a long, scary night. None of us realized that the Japanese would not be back.

Before long, Ruth decided she had better take Lovice down to bed and Sue and Mary said they were going back to their apartment, too. It was going to be a lonely night for Susie on her anniversary and Mary and Ruth were very worried about Don and Ivy. Anne, of course, had no idea where Sam was. With the phones knocked out on Ford Island, he couldn't call, but we didn't have any idea where he was. At least, I knew Frank was safe.

Anne and I didn't want to get undressed, not knowing what might happen during the night, so we just lay down on the big *hikie* (hick-ee-ay) in one corner of the living room. A *hikie* is a large, double bed-sized frame on the floor with a mattress, cover and lots of pillows on it, a useful piece of furniture in many Hawaiian homes. It makes a great place to lounge or nap in the daytime, for friendly people to gather on during a party, and it can be used as a bed at night.

As we lay there, we wondered how in the world the Japanese had been able to surprise our forces so completely. We knew that their submarines had been reported in our waters for months, but that's quite different from getting enough aircraft carriers close enough to carry out the kind of attack we'd had that morning.

We reminisced about a picnic our little group had had on a beach on windward Oahu recently. Sam and Bob had driven over the sand dunes, pretending their cars were enemy tanks. When we built a fire to cook our hot dogs, we tried to dissipate the smoke "so the enemy won't see it."

I told Anne about an evening we had spent with a Japanese businessman in a large, rather unattractive Japanese restaurant about two weeks earlier. All evening our host had apologized for our drab surroundings. He promised that "next year" he would have a very fancy dinner and evening for us.

Did he know something? Was he being prophetic, counting on rewards that might come to him if Japan took over The Islands? Probably not. A very large majority of American-Japanese in Hawaii were loyal to the U.S. as their record, both in combat and civilian life, demonstrated later throughout the war but it was an interesting question then.

We laughed, also, when I told Anne about the evening Frank and John Morris had spent with the Japanese consul general and his assistant, Otojiro Okuda. I always referred to him as "Autogiro."

About 9 o'clock we fell asleep, still fully dressed. Sometime later the sound of an airplane overhead suddenly woke us.

"Under the bed," I said.

We couldn't get under the *hikie*—it was too low—so we grabbed our pillows and rushed toward the bedroom. We wanted to get under the bed for protection from flying glass in case more bombs were coming. Suddenly I stopped, grabbing Anne's arm.

"We can't get under the bed," I said. "I haven't cleaned this week, and I know there must be dust balls under there."

This time it was Anne's turn to laugh at me. To this day, I haven't lived down that remark.

We forgot the dust balls and scrambled for safety. Nothing happened so we crawled out in a few minutes, but every time we heard a plane all night long we went under the bed again, covering our faces with pillows.

We didn't sleep much that night.

19:   The Jitters

It was going to be a jittery night for everybody.

I'd called Kay during the afternoon. She was okay—in fact, very chipper considering the situation. Anne Brown was with her as well as our immediate neighbors and they were wondering, like everyone else, what was going to happen next.

I told Kay that I wasn't going to get home that night, that we were setting up cots at the *Advertiser* and that I'd have to stay there. In fact, I wasn't sure when I was going to get home again although I'd try to make it the next morning. She assured me that she was all right and so were the rest of the girls, although worried about their men. She was a trooper. She always is when the going gets tough.

In the *Advertiser* building, as the afternoon passed, people were busy covering windows with tarpaper and anything else they could find to prevent light from leaking out. The *Advertiser's* press still was out of commission but the evening *Star-Bulletin* agreed to run its rival's morning edition on its press.

Since it was a morning paper, the *Advertiser's* staff had to work well into the night to prepare Monday's paper, then would not be able to go home because traffic was banned until dawn. The *Advertiser* brought in some folding canvas cots and Mac and I each got one and looked for suitable places to set them up. I finally found a secluded spot in a storeroom on the top floor of the three-story building where I thought I would not be disturbed if I ever got a chance to sleep.

Food was scarce and I really don't remember where what little we had came from. It couldn't have been too important at the time because there is no mention of it in my diary.

As dusk fell, what little traffic there was disappeared from Kapiolani (kap-ee-o-la-knee) Boulevard which ran past the *Advertiser* building toward Waikiki.

Inside, the *Advertiser* staff was busy getting the paper ready. In our office, Mac and I spelled each other at the teletype machine, transcribing the copy Dick Richards was picking up at the radio receiving station and relaying to us. Since it was in "cablese", a kind of news service shorthand which eliminated all unnecessary words to reduce volume on expensive overseas circuits, we had to rewrite and expand the copy as we transcribed it onto the local client circuit.

We weren't alone as Japanese targets. They also attacked the Philippines, Guam, Wake Island and Malaysia. A report from Shanghai said the Japanese were believed to have sunk or seized the U.S. liner *President Harrison* which had been scheduled to pick up U.S. Marines at Tientsin on December 10.

In London Prime Minister Winston Churchill announced a British declaration of war against Japan and Australia followed suit.

From Berlin, the German DNB news agency reported

that Japanese military headquarters in Tokyo announced that "a state of war exists from Monday at 6 a.m. between Japan and the British and U.S. forces in the Pacific." Six a.m. Monday in Tokyo was 11:30 Sunday in Honolulu, three hours and 35 minutes after the attack started.

In Washington it was announced that a U.S. army transport was torpedoed 1,300 miles west of San Francisco. In another Washington dispatch, White House Secretary Stephen Early said Japanese attacks were continuing as far as the U.S. government knew. That was more than we knew, at least as far as Honolulu was concerned.

Early said the attacks against Honolulu and Manila occurred when the U.S. and Japan "were at peace. . .and within an hour or so of the time when Nomura and Kurusu handed Secretary of State Hull the Japanese reply to Hull's November 26 memorandum."

Early also said the army received distress signals from an American vessel, presumably a cargo ship, 700 miles west of San Francisco. "This indicates that Japanese submarines are strung out over the entire area," he said.

In Honolulu, almost everybody believed the Japanese would be back. In fact, of course, the only planes which tried to fly into Hawaii that night were the six fighters from the *Enterprise* which were attacked by our own anti-aircraft gunners.

Local reports reflected the town's jitters.

Shortly after 7 p.m. the police radio ordered, "Stop all cars on Kamehameha (ka-may-ha-may-ha) Highway and Dillingham Boulevard. Defense workers are to park at the side and sleep in their cars."

Eighteen minutes later the radio instructed police to permit all cars carrying stickers properly identifying them as army or navy intelligence and FBI to proceed. That was intriguing. What were they doing? Later, we learned that some of them were picking up suspect Japanese and other aliens.

There were numerous reports of lights in various parts of town, particularly in business establishments where lights had been left on when they closed Saturday afternoon for the remainder of the weekend. "Store owners cannot drive to their stores to turn off the lights now. Crawl through a transom, if necessary, to get at the switch, or shoot them out," the radio told patrolmen.

As the night wore on fatigue overcame tension. Mac and I divided the night into shifts, one of us manning the office while the other napped. When it came my turn to try to sleep, I retired to my hideaway on the third floor.

It was totally dark up there and I had a hard time finding my cot. When I finally did, I shucked off my clothes except for my shorts, lay down and spread the clothes over me in lieu of covers.

But sleep would not come. Too many things ran through my mind. How had we done on the story? Usually, on a big story like this, messages come in from the general desk in New York with suggestions, complaints or compliments, but the navy had shut off communications too soon so we didn't know.

What was coming next? How could the three of us cover it? For that matter, would we survive it?

I tried to doze but it wasn't much use. Then it began to get hot. Because of the blackout, every door and window in the building was tightly shut. Hawaiian nights usually are delightful but a buttoned-up building housing a hundred or more people and a lot of machinery, including pots melting lead for linotypes and casting machines, can get pretty warm. Finally, I got up and dressed. Nearby was a short flight of stairs leading to the roof. I climbed them and stepped out into the dark night.

The Jitters

The moon was gone and it was pitch black under gathering clouds. At first, it was impossible to see anything. I could hear some voices. As my eyes became accustomed to the gloom, I made out a few figures. Others couldn't sleep either.

Someone started to light a cigarette. Someone else said, "Douse it. We can't show any lights up here."

There was more to his caution than a desire to observe the blackout rules. Occasionally we'd hear the sharp *crack* of a rifle. Soldiers patrolling the streets were jittery too. Any light, any movement might draw a rifle or pistol bullet.

I suppose our conversation was typical of many in Honolulu that night. There was talk of the sneakiness of the attack, of getting "those little yellow bastards", of what really had happened at Pearl, Hickam, Wheeler and the other bases, of the rumors we'd all heard of arrows in the canefields, Hawaiian class rings on dead Japanese pilots, contaminated water and parachutists in the hills.

It was a depressing conversation. Whatever the truth was, it was obvious that the navy and air corps had suffered grievous damage. Nobody knew what might happen next. Would the Japanese planes be back? Would the Japanese follow up with a landing? If they did, would they strike directly at Oahu with its major navy, army and air corps bases or would they land first on one or more of the outer islands—Maui, Kauai, Molokai or the Big Island of Hawaii?

Fortunately for us, the Japanese plan did not include an attempt to capture Hawaii. They lost an opportunity that would not be repeated.

It was time to get back to work, to relieve Mac downstairs. The sky was beginning to lighten but it had turned drizzly and even seemed to be chilly for Honolulu. It was not a dawn to lift our depressed spirits.

20: "Saboteurs Land Here"

The *Advertiser's* Monday morning edition did nothing to calm the situation.

"SABOTEURS LAND HERE," screamed its two-line banner across the top of page one. The letters were nearly three inches high.

"Raiders Return in Dawn Attack," it shouted in inch-high type over a three-column lead story.

"Renewed Japanese bombing attacks on Oahu were reported as Honolulu woke to the sound of anti-aircraft fire in a cold, drizzling dawn today," the story said. "Patrons were warned to be on the watch for parachutists reported in Kalini (ka-lee-nee—a residential district).

"Red anti-aircraft bursts shot into the cloudy skies from the direction of Hickam Field which was reported bombed again about 6 a.m. Brief machine gun firing was heard from several points downtown and along the waterfront as American planes soared low over the city toward the east.

"Warning that a party of saboteurs had been landed on

98

northern Oahu was given early Sunday afternoon by the army. The saboteurs were distinguished by red disks on their shoulders."

The army did report an air raid just before dawn but withdrew the report later when the planes proved to be American, perhaps Sam Brown's scout planes heading out to look for the Japanese fleet. Later in the day, the army announced that no Japanese air raids of any kind had occurred in the Hawaiian Islands after "the sporadic raids of early Sunday night."

In fact, there were no Japanese raids after the second wave of attacking planes completed their mission shortly before 10 a.m. Sunday. The reports of raids Sunday night probably stemmed from our own action against the unfortunate pilots of Fighting Six from the *Enterprise*.

There were no "saboteurs" either but reports about them were persistent as were reports of parachutists landing at various places on the island. Several such reports appeared on army communications channels during the day Sunday including the one Mac had included in one of his reports. Like the others, it proved to be erroneous.

Years later, while visiting the editor of a Southern California newspaper, I was embarrassed to find a slip of yellow UP teletype copy among various other pieces of copy thumbtacked on the wall behind his desk. "Flash—Parachutists land on Oahu." It said. "That's my 'Bloopers corner,'" the editor said, laughing at my embarrassment.

Another report had "parachutists landing on Tantalus," a 2,000 foot mountain behind Honolulu. Investigation found no parachutists there either.

Harry Albright, in his book *Pearl Harbor, Japan's Fatal Blunder* tells of an excited call which reported, "The Japanese are landing at Kawela Bay." The G-2 officer who received the call at Fort Shafter knew that no military observation post had reported enemy surface craft off Oahu's northern shore where Kawela Bay is located. "Are you certain of your information?" He asked. "Hell, man, I can see the sunlight flashing on their bayonets!" came back the answer. But like the parachutists and saboteurs, the landing troops also were non-existent.(7)

When there is a lack of factual information, gossip and rumor, even deliberate misinformation, tends to fill the void. We were not aware of any deliberate attempts by anyone to spread false information in Hawaii, but of gossip and rumor there was a great deal. Still, the reasons for censorship were obvious. The American fleet had been crippled seriously, our air forces on Oahu were nearly annihilated. While the Japanese pilots returning to their carriers knew they had scored heavily, they could not be certain of the extent of the damage. Although we reporters fretted and fussed, I came to realize later that the navy was correct, under the circumstances, to impose censorship as quickly as it could on outgoing communications.

You never want to let the enemy know how badly you've been hurt, but neither the army nor navy was any better prepared that Sunday morning to censor the flow of information than they were to repel the Japanese. In the face of that lack of preparedness, a temporary total blackout of outgoing news was understandable. In fact, it was the only sensible course of action.

But why they tried to cut off all incoming news as well was not understandable. Whether they believed that some instructions might reach possible Japanese saboteurs or espionage agents or what their motive was, I never was able to learn. It may simply have been a knee-jerk, protective reaction.

What the navy risked, however, was adding to the

possibility of panic and hysteria in a jittery community. Had it not been for the United Press receiving station which continued to bring in our report for the local news media, Hawaii would not have known what was being done and said in Washington and other world capitals.

It would not have known what President Roosevelt told Congress on Monday, nor that Congress passed a Declaration of War with one dissenting vote, that the country was mobilizing to avenge Pearl Harbor, that the Free World was expressing its outrage and indignation over Japan's sneak attack. Aside from the UP reports, the only news from outside came at night when some radios could pick up the powerful, 50,000-watt stations in San Francisco and Los Angeles.

I never knew, either, why the navy, having closed down all the commercial communications companies, didn't close down our receiving station, too. They certainly knew it was there since it was on open land between PearlHarbor and Ewa and military aircraft flew over it every day. Maybe they did realize the importance of incoming news and left us alone deliberately since our station handled nothing but our own incoming traffic and had no transmitter.

Of course, rumor was not confined to Hawaii. Apparently it was abroad in Washington as well in the absence of solid information.

Bill, Mac and I were puzzled and concerned to read the main UP war lead out of Washington Monday morning which said, "The United States pressed huge scale naval and aerial operations against Japan in the Battle of the Pacific today, Washington sources reported.

"The United State's counteroffensive began at the moment the first Japanese bomb exploded in Hawaii, according to the naval officials.

"Immediate objectives of the Pacific and Asiatic fleets were to hunt down marauding Japanese naval units in the Pacific and blockade Japan, cutting off, if possible, all approaches to Japan from the sea. . . .

"No details regarding the United States' action were divulged and only the general statement was made that the United States Navy was striking with all the forces at its command. . . ."

Who were those sources which reported huge naval and aerial operations? There in Honolulu, we didn't know where the *Enterprise* and *Lexington* were, but we knew the navy had suffered a grievous blow in Pearl Harbor. We knew that some ships had left the harbor—I'd reported that myself when I saw a few destroyers steaming to sea through the channel next to Hickam Sunday morning—but we knew there wasn't much of a fleet immediately available, certainly not one capable of fighting a major naval battle.

What we learned later was that the ships which escaped Pearl Harbor—mostly destroyers and light cruisers—joined Halsey's *Enterprise* task force. Kimmel ordered Halsey and the *Lexington* group to rendezvous as soon as possible with Vice Admiral Brown's scouting force of cruisers and destroyers which had been operating near Johnston Island to the southwest and with the three old battleships and their escorts which had been part of the *Enterprise's* original force.

For the moment, those ships, Oahu's big coast artillery guns and two army divisions were the only defense Hawaii had if the Japanese armada returned. But it didn't, and there was no big naval battle going on either.

21 : "We Were Scared" (Kay)

The early morning sunlight spreading across the *hikie* told Anne and me it was time to end our fitful dozing. Although we hadn't had much sleep, we welcomed the dawn. I frighten more easily in the dark.

The news on the radio as we showered and dressed brought some relief from immediate fright but made us want to cry. The Japanese apparently had gone but damage was heavy although censorship prevented the reporting of many specifics. There must have been many casualties and we could guess that there wasn't much left with which to defend The Islands.

We faced an uncertain future and, frankly, we were scared. We'd read too much about Japanese atrocities in China, not just against the military but also against civilians—the young, the old, male and female—to be anything else.

The radio also told us something about what life was

going to be like for awhile. Gasoline was strictly rationed and civilians were told to hold driving to an absolute minimum. Grocery stores were open but were instructed to sell only normal amounts to regular customers to prevent hoarders from stripping their shelves. Liquor sales were suspended indefinitely.

Later in the day, the governor ordered food stores to close Tuesday to take inventory so the authorities could get a better idea of just how much food was available for the civilian population. Hawaii imported most of its food and who knew when we would get new shipments

Just as we were ready to sit down to breakfast, Frank came through the door. He was tired, gaunt and unshaven, but there he was.

Anne was so glad to see him that she burst into tears. She was so worried about Sam that just seeing Frank suddenly appear broke a dam of emotion.

Frank had no specific news of the New Orleans but he knew the names of the ships which had been most seriously damaged and she was not among them. Neither were the Sothard nor the Detroit, so Bob and Don might be okay, but he didn't know anything about Ivy's ship.

While we set another place and prepared more food, Frank showered, shaved and put on fresh clothes. He had to go back to the office as soon as possible.

Over breakfast we discussed what we should do next. Since a number of what we had thought were bombs had fallen nearby the day before, and since we were in an exposed position if the Japanese returned for a naval bombardment, Frank thought that Anne and I should find a safer location.

After some phone calls, Anne arranged to join Janet Hahn, the wife of one of Sam's shipmates, who was staying with a neighbor in Manoa valley. That left Janet's house, also in Manoa, vacant so Janet said that Susie, Mary and I could go there. Frank said he had to sleep at the office again that night and Ruth decided that she and Lovice would stay on Alewa Heights. She wanted to be there in case there was a call about Ivy.

Transportation was a problem because the Brown, Davidson and Hahn cars all were in Pearl Harbor and Frank had to have ours at the office. Help appeared, however, in the person of Priscilla Cotton, a friend visiting from the mainland, who drove up to see how we all had fared. She would assist our exodus.

Since Frank was in a hurry to get back to the bureau, I began throwing things indiscriminately into our car. I emptied the refrigerator of all our food because I had no idea how long we'd be at Janet's nor when I could shop. I also threw in practically all my daytime clothing and finally declared that I was ready.

Anne was laughing at me again. "Kate (as she called me) packed practically all her possessions," she wrote in her diary. "It was so funny." Well, Anne was traveling light. Frank says I never have.

Priscilla took Anne and Frank drove me, Sue and Mary to Janet's. We unloaded quickly and said good-bye again to Frank. He said he would try to join us Tuesday night.

The daylight hours flew by. This time, we began to plan dinner well in advance and we took stock of our available food early. We discovered that the lettuce had begun to turn brown and we debated for some time whether the brown stuff would hurt us or not. Despite my reputation with Anne, I really was not an experienced kitchen mechanic, even after more that two years of marriage.

Susie and Mary were no better than I but we decided to heck with it, we'd eat it anyway. The possibility of getting more any time soon seemed pretty remote right then. Fortunately, we had a pretty good supply of canned food as well as some perishables, so we thought we could get by all right, at least until Wednesday when the stores were supposed to reopen.

We had considerably more freedom of movement at Janet's house because it had both shades and drapes in some rooms which could be drawn to keep light from showing in the blackout.

Anne and Janet walked over after dinner and we all decided that we had to talk about something different tonight. By this time, we had learned that most of the rumors were true about the battleships being sunk at Pearl Harbor and most of our air fleet being destroyed on the ground.

Our situation was just too depressing to talk about any more, so we spent the evening reviewing world history, at least as we remembered it. I don't believe any of us qualified as a scholar of history, but it was better than more worrying about current events.

We went to bed early again, about 9 o'clock, not as worried as the night before, but still jumpy and uncertain.

22: Declaration of War

As I drove through downtown en route home and then back to the office again from Manoa Valley, Honolulu was a mixture of "business as usual" and a military camp.

Traffic was close to normal and most stores were open, but armed and helmeted soldiers guarded Hawaiian Electric, the telephone company and a number of other buildings. Other troops strung barbed wire and set up gun emplacements near the waterfront and Iolani Palace.

At the office, the story was in on President Roosevelt's address to Congress and the White House official statement on the Pearl Harbor attack. The first was a stirring call to arms, the second a pretty misleading account of the catastrophe.

"Yesterday, December 7, 1941—a date which will live in infamy—the United States of America was suddenly and deliberately attacked by naval and air forces of the Empire of Japan," the President said.

107

It took him only six and a half minutes to summarize Sunday's events and to ask Congress to "declare that since the unprovoked and dastardly attack by Japan on Sunday, December 7, 1941, a state of war has existed between the United States and the Japanese Empire."

He noted that the United States was at peace and, "at the solicitation of Japan, was still in conversation with its government and its Emperor looking toward the maintenance of peace in the Pacific."

He said the bombing began an hour before Nomura and Kurusu delivered their document to Hull and that it was "obvious that the attack was deliberately planned many days or even weeks ago. During the intervening time, the Japanese government has deliberately sought to deceive the United States by false statements and expressions of hope for continued peace."

The President said the attack caused severe damage, that many lives were lost in Hawaii and that Japanese also attacked Malaya, Hong Kong, Guam, the Philippines, Wake Island and Midway Island in a "surprise offensive extending throughout the Pacific area. . . .

"No matter how long it may take us to overcome this premeditated invasion, the American people, in their righteous might, will win through to absolute victory. . . .

"There is no blinking the fact that our people, our territory and our interests are in grave danger.

"With confidence in our armed forces, with the unbounding determination of our people, we will gain the inevitable triumph. So help us God."(8)

The Congress, meeting in joint session in the presence of the Cabinet and Supreme Court, cheered the President repeatedly during his brief address. Only 33 minutes after he finished, the Senate approved a resolution declaring that a state of war exists between Japan and the United States by a vote of 82 to 0 the House by 388 to 1. Miss Jeanette Rankin, a Republican from Montana, was the lone dissenter. She also had voted against entering World War I.

The official White House résumé of the attack was not very informative for the American public and, for those like ourselves who had at least a general ideal of the dimensions of the disaster, it seemed to be downright misleading. Of course, it was meant to mislead the Japanese but their claims, as broadcast from Tokyo today, were a lot closer to the mark than Washington's.

The White House, after saying that "operations against the Japanese attacking force in the neighborhood of the Hawaiian Islands are still continuing," reported, "The damage caused to our forces in Oahu in yesterday's attack appears more serious than at first believed.

"In Pearl Harbor itself one old battleship has capsized and several other ships have been seriously damaged.

"One destroyer was blown up, several other small ships were seriously hurt. Army and navy fields were bombed with the resulting destruction of several hangars. A large number of planes were put out of commission."

The report said casualties on Oahu "in all probability, will amount to about 3,000. Nearly half of those are fatalities, the others being wounded. It seems clear from the report that many bombs were dropped in the city of Honolulu, resulting in a small number of causalities."

The last part of that sentence was correct, the first part wrong, although at the time, we all thought that the city had taken bomb hits, not hits from our own defective or misdirected anti-aircraft shells.

The "old battleship" which capsized presumably was

the target ship *Utah*. The report of damage to the navy was a far cry from the facts and from what Japanese pilots must have observed, given the success of their attack from its first moments.

Meanwhile, we sat there knowing that at least five of our battleships were sunk or, if some were not sunk technically, they were so badly wrecked that they could only sit on the shallow bottom. We knew that other ships also were seriously damaged and that few of our military aircraft remained.

I still have copies of cables we had prepared for filing when censorship permitted. One says, in the cablese we used, that the attack "reportedly sank five battleships pearlharbor afired fueltanks wrecked other installations stop four exeight hangars hickam field alongside pearlharbor received direct hits planes both field hangars damaged stop. . .bombs dropped close barracks hickam estimated casualties there highs threefifty. . .

"armys wheelerfield next schofieldbarracks reportedly badly hit understood planes there undispersed wherefore single bombhits wrecked many however some pforties [P-40 fighters] took off. . . ."

The copy bears the handwritten notation, "No/SBR.: "SBR" was Lieutenant Samuel B. (Buck) Riddick, the 14th Naval District Public Information Officer who was drafted for collateral duty as a censor when the Navy finally let us send something, although not much, on Thursday, December 11.

The Japanese broadcasts today, however, were reporting that they had sunk two battleships and a minesweeper and severely damaged four other capital ships and four cruisers. The two battleships certainly were the *Arizona* and *Oklahoma*, whose deaths many of the Japanese pilots must have seen.

The four capital ships heavily damaged would have been the battleships *Nevada, West Virginia, California* and *Maryland.* The Japanese claimed the destruction of only "about 100 American planes" in Hawaii, the Philippines and Guam, well below what they got on Oahu alone, one justification, I suppose, for the White House not being more forthcoming in its announcement.

Two weeks later, on December 16, Secretary of the Navy Frank Knox was a little more realistic upon returning to Washington from a four-day visit to Pearl Harbor. Reporters never saw him while he was there, but at a press conference immediately upon his return to the capital, he delivered a report which put the best possible light on the situation.

He said the Japanese failed to achieve their objective of knocking out the United States before the war began, but he admitted the loss of the battleship *Arizona,* the destroyers *Cassin, Downes* and *Shaw* and the minelayer *Oglala.*

He said damage to other vessels "varies from ships which will take from a few weeks to several months to repair. In this last category is the older battleship *Oklahoma,* which has been capsized but which can be righted and repaired.

"The entire balance of the Pacific fleet with its aircraft carriers, its heavy cruisers, its light cruisers, its destroyers and submarines, are uninjured and are all at sea seeking contact with the enemy."

Under questioning, he said he should have included battleships among the warships at sea but the fact was that the only ones at sea were the three slow old battlewagons Halsey had left behind when he made his high speed run to Wake.

A radio broadcast of Knox's press conference was heard on the *Enterprise* as she patrolled north of Oahu. The log of Fighting Six noted facetiously, "SecNav came over the air with the details that only one BB [battleship] was sunk in Pearl Harbor. Very encouraging, very encouraging."

Of the eight battleships which actually were sunk or damaged, the *Pennsylvania* returned to action in short order. The *Arizona* was gone and the *Oklahoma* never was repaired. The other five, saved by the shallow bottom, did come back months later.

A year later, the navy issued an anniversary communiqué in which it admitted that the Japanese had "temporarily disabled every battleship and most of the aircraft in the Hawaiian area.

"Other naval vessels, both combatant and auxiliary, were put out of action, and certain shore facilities, especially at the army air bases, Hickam and Wheeler Fields, and the naval air stations, Ford Island and Kaneone Bay, were damaged. Most of these ships are now back with the fleet. The aircraft all were replaced within a few days and interference with facilities was generally limited to a matter of hours."

The communiqué said the five battleships, the *Arizona, Oklahoma, California, Nevada* and *West Virginia*; three destroyers, the *Shaw, Cassin* and *Downes'*; the minelayer *Oglala*, the target ship *Utah* and a large floating drydock were either sunk or damaged so severely that they would serve no military purposes for some time.

The communiqué prompted Bob Casey, the respected foreign correspondent of the Chicago Daily News to quip "the navy announced today that five of the two battleships sunk at Pearl Harbor have been raised."

The communiqué said the most serious losses were American lives. It said that 3,303 were killed, died of their wounds or were still missing and that 1,272 were wounded, a total of 4,573 men and women.

23: Japan's Mistakes

While Washington dispatches were reporting that America was fighting back against Japanese sea and air forces in a spreading Battle of the Pacific, the distance between the two fleets in the central Pacific actually was growing greater by the hour.

Halsey, low on oil in the *Enterprise*, and his escort vessels had to refuel. The *Lexington* task force and Vice Admiral Wilson Brown's scouting force were en route to rendezvous with Halsey. They weren't chasing anybody, didn't even know where the enemy was.

To the northwest, the big Japanese fleet, its carrier-borne air groups almost unscathed after their historic victory at Pearl Harbor, steamed homeward. With them went a never-to-be-repeated opportunity to deal the United States a blow from which it might never have recovered. The attack on Pearl Harbor was a huge success for Japan but Japan made four mistakes. They were its undoing:

1. Their plan did not include invasion of Hawaii.
2. They left Pearl Harbor's huge oil tank farm undamaged, leaving the surviving fleet fuel on which to operate.

3. They did not attack the navy yard's vulnerable support and repair facilities. Consequently, the navy was able to begin repairing damaged ships immediately, to repair ships damaged in future actions, and to support the operations of its very effective submarine fleet, also left undamaged
4. They united an America then not ready to go to war. This, coupled with their failure to administer the coup de grace on December 7, resulted in their ultimate defeat.

In addition, destruction of the so-called battleline, the slow old battleships, may have been a blessing in disguise. As Sam Brown told the exec on the *New Orleans* that morning, "Don't cry, Commander, we still have airplanes."

That may have made the commander cry harder, but now there would be no argument about letting the speedy carriers operate in fast task forces supported only by equally speedy cruisers and destroyers.

This changed concepts of naval warfare. America's fast carrier task forces never lost an engagement in World War II. Their bombers prepared Japanese-held islands for invasion and, finally, with the B-29's, they wreaked havoc in the Japanese homeland in 1945.

U.S. battleships, used mostly as artillery platforms to soften up invasion targets, never played a major role in a Pacific naval engagement.

Had the Japanese plans included invasion, there was nothing to prevent their landing on any of the outside islands of Hawaii, Maui, Kauai, Molokai or Lanai where there were virtually no defenses. On Oahu, there were two army divisions, the 24th and 25th, but almost all of the island's landbased aircraft had been destroyed.

Oahu was heavily equipped with various kinds of artillery.

There were 127 coastal artillery pieces including some 16-inch guns designed to blast an enemy fleet if it got close enough. The army had over 200 anti-aircraft guns in various locations supplemented by the navy's at Pearl Harbor and Kaneohe and there were more than 3,000 artillery pieces and automatic weapons to defend the beaches.

Except for some anti-aircraft and automatic weapons damaged at the navy yard and air fields, this equipment was intact. However, it is doubtful that even with this support the two army divisions and the comparatively small American naval force left in Hawaiian waters could have held off a determined Japanese invasion long enough for significant help to arrive.

Only a few weeks earlier, in November, I'd interviewed General Short on the state of the territory's military readiness. I'd asked him what would happen if Japan tried to take Hawaii:

"We'd probably lose the outside islands," he said, "but I believe we could hold Oahu."

I took him at his word then but in later years, after I'd seen the Japanese fortifications, the networks of tunnels and the armament that American Marines and GIs had to overcome to take island after island in their march across the Pacific, I realized that Oahu's defenses in 1941 were not in the same class. I decided that Short had been talking for effect or had been unrealistically optimistic.

Of course, when we had our interview, he had not anticipated losing virtually all his air power and the navy's battleline in one sneak attack, but even before that terrible morning, the landbased forces of his command were relatively weak.

Late in December, after a number of correspondents had arrived from The States to augment the news service staffs and to represent some of the major newspapers, the army conducted a press tour of its facilities on Oahu. We visited the big coastal artillery installations, beach defenses, gun emplacements, and units in the field.

The tour was designed to impress us with Oahu's readiness to repel invasion, if it came. But after comparing what we saw then with what Americans found at Guadalcanal, Tarawa, Saipan, Guam, Iwo Jima and Okinawa, Oahu's defenses seemed pretty puny.

The tour also took us to some of the bases the Japanese hit on December 7. Even then, three weeks later, the devastation was impressive. Someone asked Bob Casey of the Chicago *Daily News*, who had just arrived in Honolulu after covering the first two years of the war in Europe, how the damage at Wheeler Field compared with what the Nazis' had done to Rotterdam. "Total destruction looks the same the world over," said Bob.

Casey and H.R. Knickerbocker of the Chicago *Sun*, the first correspondents from the mainland to reach Honolulu, had arrived on a dingy old tramp steamer, the first transportation they could get from the West Coast.

"We proved there wasn't a Jap sub between California and Hawaii," Bob said. "That ship smoked all day and threw sparks all night."

While both Wheeler and Hickam Fields, as well as the navy air stations on Ford Island and at Kaneohe Bay, had been badly hit, they were functioning and able to support the replacement aircraft which had arrived within days after December 7.

But most important, the big navy yard at Pearl Harbor hardly missed a beat.

My censored copy which said Japanese bombs "afired fuel tanks" was wrong. The attackers apparently never even tried to bomb the huge fuel tank farm at Pearl and they barely touched the ship repair facilities there, sinking only a floating drydock.

That made it possible for the yard to return many of the less seriously damaged ships to the fleet in short order and it meant that the fleet had fuel on which to operate.

Invasion of Hawaii was not part of the Japanese grand stategy which was focused on Southeast Asia. Their objective at Pearl Harbor was to neutralize the Pacific Fleet so it could not interfere. Good fortune on the American side and a planning flaw on the Japanese side prevented their achieving that objective fully.

Part of the American good fortune was that the aircraft carrier *Saratoga* was on the West Coast for repairs and the *Lexington* and *Enterprise* were at sea so none of them came under attack.

The flaw in the Japanese planning was that they concentrated on the old battleships and left the navy yard's huge oil tank farm and repair facilities alone.

On December 7, 1958, Admiral Chester W. Nimitz, who succeeded Kimmel and directed the Allied assault across the Pacific, wrote about that mistake in *The American Weekly*, the Hearst newspaper supplement.(9) He pointed out that the Japanese could have returned to "methodically and leisurely. . .destroy the repair facilities of the naval base and to burn—with explosive machine gun fire—4,500,000 barrels of fuel oil stored in a completely exposed tank farm.

"What a shocking loss that would have been," he continued. "The destruction of the repair facilities would have forced our navy all the way back to the West Coast of the United States.

"The loss of that great fuel supply would have been well nigh irreparable. The campaigns against the Japanese would have been so much delayed that they might have established themselves strongly in the Western Pacific and years of effort would be needed for their expulsion. . . .

"What happened instead was perhaps the greatest boon and good luck to come to our navy out of our misfortune at Pearl Harbor. Because we were caught by surprise, our fleet was in a relatively shallow port. This fact enabled us to salvage most of our outdated ships and greatly reduce the loss of our trained officers and men. . . .

"The object of the Japanese attack on Pearl Harbor was to inflict sufficient damage to our naval strength to give their navy a free hand to expand and consolidate its holdings. For this purpose, they could have chosen better targets at Pearl Harbor—the destruction of its fuel.

"The Japanese attack left our submarine base at Pearl virtually untouched. Its destruction by bombs would have been easy and it would have greatly hampered our most effective—and only—available weapon, our submarine force, which, incidentally, was the only force we had which could operate unsupported in Japanese waters from the earliest days of the war. . . .

"Just why the Japanese Navy failed to complete the havoc and destruction at Pearl Harbor, which was easily in their power, must be left to another story.

"But the attack shocked our country out of its apathy about the World War already under way in Europe. All the arguments for and against entering the conflict ended and America, as one man, joined the fight against aggression."

As Nimitz noted, our submarines were untouched in the attack and the effects of their forays into the Western Pacific became apparent within a few weeks with reports of enemy ships being sunk.

It didn't take long for the carriers to get into action either, although their task forces were kept on patrol duty in Hawaiian waters for the first few weeks of the war. The first carrier foray, however, was aborted, apparently by a Japanese sub.

On January 6, a month after the Pearl Harbor attack, I went to sea aboard the heavy cruiser *Indianapolis* with a task force headed west. We never were told what our objective was and we returned to Pearl eight days later, reportedly because an aircraft carrier, probably the *Saratoga*, "took a fish"—was damaged by a torpedo.

However, on February 1, a task force led by the carriers *Enterprise* and *Yorktown* landed America's first blow of retaliation in a bombing attack on Japanese facilities in the Marshall and Gilbert Islands. The navy claimed 15 to 17 Japanese ships and 41 planes destroyed and shore bases damaged. Neither of those operations would have been possible had the Japanese gone after the fuel tanks on December 7.

Even more important, the navy yard's undamaged repair capability played a crucial part in the navy's success only six months later at the Battle of Midway, the first major turning point in the war.

In that battle on June 4, 5 and 6, three U.S. carriers and their task forces supported by army and Marine war planes from Midway, turned back a superior Japanese force bent on capturing the island preparatory to a return to Hawaii.

Throughout the battle, the opposing ships never saw each other but fliers from the U.S. carriers and Midway sank four Japanese carriers, two heavy cruisers, three destroyers and one or more transports. The Japanese lost at least 275 planes, and three battleships and a number of other ships were damaged.

Prominent in that battle were the planes from the

Yorktown which had been seriously damaged in the Battle of the Coral Sea May 4-8, 1942, America's first naval victory of the war. The *Yorktown* limped into Pearl Harbor on the afternoon of May 27, so badly damaged that it should have taken three months to return her to service.

Instead, the hundreds of navy yard service and civilian workers who swarmed over her day and night sent her back to sea on the morning of May 30. Four days later she joined the *Enterprise* and *Hornet* in an ambush that sent the Japanese attackers home in defeat, never again to return to the Central Pacific.

The *Yorktown* herself was sunk in the battle, but she never would have been there had the Japanese given some of their attention to Pearl Harbor's repair facilities on December 7.

24: A New Way of Life

On Monday morning, December 8, it did not seem to us that the Japanese had made any mistakes.

At that point, we did not know that the navy yard's repair facilities had suffered little damage and that the fuel tank farm was intact. We didn't know anything about the two U.S. carrier task forces at sea and we didn't know where the Japanese were or what they might do next.

All we knew was that our fleet and aircraft had suffered grievous losses, much more than Washington was admitting. We believed we were sitting ducks if the Japanese came back.

That they would come back seemed inevitable. Except for some visible signs of preparation, we had no idea what the army and navy might be doing to prepare for that.

The visible signs were the troops stringing barbed wire in some areas, principally near the waterfront, and setting up anti-aircraft guns and machine gun nests. At Waikiki and along other beaches, they laid out great rolls of barbed wire to impede enemy landing forces.

Outside the city, troops worked feverishly to prepare for what everyone assumed would be the coming onslaught.

The 24th and 25th Divisions had moved into the field Sunday, hurriedly taking their assigned positions. Now the work of strengthening their defenses continued. The sandbag emplacements and barbed wire entanglements we saw in the city and on nearby beaches were duplicated and multiplied all over the island.

Tanks rumbled into positions from which they could engage an advancing enemy. Camouflage netting concealed some of them as well as various other positions.

Ammunition trucks rolled out from big underground storage dumps to infantry and artillery stations along the shore and in the mountains. When the blow fell, it would be preceded by air strikes followed by naval bombardment so antiaircraft gunners and the crews of the huge coastal artillery rifles stood ready.

What patrol aircraft were left, such as Sam Brown's seaplane scouts, were in the air but there were so few of them that an approaching enemy naval force might easily escape their notice. If it didn't, its carrier-borne fighters would overwhelm the remaining handful of American fighters.

But in Honolulu, there was a false air of near normalcy.

At 7 a.m., Edouard Doty, Territorial Director of Civil Defense, announced that business downtown "will continue as usual" and most establishments opened at their normal hours or soon thereafter. They were instructed to close at 4:30 p.m. so employees and customers could get home before blackout.

Doty warned people to use automobiles as sparingly as possible and to take busses instead. Later in the day, he told service stations to limit customers to half a tankful of gas. That restriction soon was replaced by a ration of 10 gallons per car per month except for defense workers and others with essential jobs.

The Territory was under martial law proclaimed by Governor Poindexter Sunday after which General Short took over as military governor, but many instructions continued to come from Poindexter's office.

To head off price-gouging on the one hand and hoarding on the other, Poindexter ordered that the dealers in food or feed shall not sell more of these commodities than is normally their practice and that no one shall sell any such supplies to anyone not his regular customer.

"This means that you may buy from your regular supplier in your customary amounts, but no more," his order said. He ordered police to arrest any store owners who refused to sell food to the public.

During the morning, reports came in of some store owners who refused to sell food at all and of Japanese stores which would sell only to Japanese. Police were detailed to order shopkeepers to conduct their businesses as usual and to arrest any who refused.

In the afternoon, a Japanese Chamber of Commerce official said the reports about the Japanese stores were misunderstandings. He said hundreds of buyers rushed some of the stores so, to keep order, the owners closed their doors and permitted only their own customers to enter single file.

Later, Poindexter ordered all grocery stores, importers, wholesalers, retailers and other food dealers to close Tuesday, December 9 and remain closed until licensed to

123

reopen. He said the licenses would be issued Wednesday after the establishments had completed inventories of stocks on hand.

An evacuation zone for some blocks back from the waterfront and beach areas had been established and Poindexter told residents of those areas that they could move to the University of Hawaii or any of the public schools *mauka* (mau-ka—toward the hills) of the downtown area if they wished. Few did, however.

He ordered schools closed until further notice but instructed city, county and territorial employees to report for work as usual unless ordered otherwise. Federal employees also went to work.

"To the best of our knowledge, civilian casualties amounted to 182 cases now hospitalized," Poindexter said. "The exact count of dead and wounded is not yet complete. . . .

"Everything is being done by the military and civil authorities to insure your well being. In turn, you are expected to obey orders unquestioningly and to keep calm."

The manager of the Honolulu waterworks Frederick Ohrt rescinded Sunday's order to boil water and conserve a supply in bathtubs after laboratory tests showed the water supply was not contaminated. That set to rest one of Sunday's most persistent rumors, but he said if there was another attack, bathtubs and other containers should be filled in case mains and feeder pipes were ruptured.

Pedestrians crowded the downtown business section and Waikiki's shopping area during the day much as usual and the department stores and specialty shops seemed to be doing a lively Christmas business.

But along with all this, there was tension in the air and

anger and determination in every conversation. There was little evidence of panic but a lot of talk about getting the job done and going after "those sneaky yellow bastards." There was wonder over how the military could have been caught so sound asleep.

In a Pearl Harbor anniversary story he wrote for United Press 20 years later, Howard Case, the *Star-Bulletin* city editor, said, "The most vivid memory I have of that December 7 was the amazing recovery of the people of Hawaii. Everybody worked together and we had a combined military government and civilian government. We had to have the military fighting for us, and the military had to depend on the civilians for their support. It was a good combination and it worked."

One of the first things the military government did was to halt all civil court functions temporarily and transfer the courts' powers to military courts. That meant that the privilege of *habeas corpus* was suspended and that defendants could be tried under the regulations of special or summary courts martial.

The assistant military governor, Lieutenant Colonel Thomas H. Green, who functioned throughout the war as the territory's *de facto* governor, said sentences ordinarily would not exceed the limits of punishment prescribed by territorial or federal law. "However, the courts are not bound by these limits," he warned.

When the courts reopened as military courts, most of the first cases had to do with blackout violations and similar infractions. Two violators were fined $10 each but in two other cases, described as "more flagrant", the violators were fined $100 each and sentenced to 100 days at hard labor as "enemies of the territory." The hard labor sentences were suspended later.

There was a fascinating little item in the *Star-Bulletin* which said that a program sponsored by the Honolulu United Japanese Society for 9:30 a.m. Sunday went ahead as scheduled at the *Kokusai* theater. That would have been at the height of the attack by the second wave of Japanese warplanes.

At the ceremony, 800 Japanese-speaking emergency medical volunteers were presented with certificates for completion of their basic Red Cross first aid training. The story didn't say whether the volunteers then offered their services to hospitals where, by that time, the wounded were pouring in, but it said the Society urged all Japanese in the Islands to remain calm.

Perhaps the first civilian to become aware of the attack was attorney Roy Vitousek who was flying his own plane near the Honolulu airport early Sunday. He said some of the attacking planes came so close to him that he could identify the pilots as Japanese.

Vitousek landed quickly. As his plane taxied up to the parking area, he said he saw a Japanese plane swoop in low over the field, machine guns blazing, and cut down Bob Tyce, operator of a flying service, who was about to pull the prop to start his plane.

The army and navy would say nothing about the Japanese attack and the communications blackout would have prevented us sending anything anyway. However, as we and the *Advertiser* staff checked around town, bits and pieces of information began to turn up in addition to what we already knew about the devastation at Pearl Harbor and the air bases. There were several reports about warnings early Sunday which never reached command level.

The first concerned the destroyer *Ward* which Kay later

saw dodging bombs from a Japanese plane offshore. There was a rumor going around that the *Ward* had actually sunk a Japanese submarine just outside Pearl Harbor before the enemy planes ever appeared.

Later, the story was confirmed during the Pearl Harbor investigations. The *Ward* was on patrol duty all night, covering a two-mile-square area off the entrance to Pearl Harbor. At about 6:30 a.m., she received a report from the supply ship *Antares,* preparing to enter the harbor, that she had sighted a suspicious-looking object, possibly a submarine.

The *Ward* sped to the scene and her helmsman spotted what appeared to be the conning tower of a submarine probably preparing to follow the *Antares* into the harbor. The *Ward* closed rapidly to about 50 yards from the intruder and opened fire.(10)

She promptly scored a hit and the submarine keeled over. Then the *Ward* propped a pattern of depth charges which apparently sank the sub.

The *Ward's* commander, Lieutenant William W. Outerbridge, reported the action to 14th Naval District headquarters at 6:53 a.m. Then followed a series of phone calls and consultations among officers of the 14th Naval District and Pacific Fleet headquarters to assess the reliability and implications of the report. Meanwhile, the navy sent out no aerial patrols, the army was not notified and there was no change in the alert status of either the army or navy.(11)

Another story concerned a boy on a motorbike, a Commercial Cable Company messenger. He was trying to deliver a warning message from Army Chief of Staff General George C. Marshall in Washington to General Short at Fort Shafter. Although the warning might have been too late to have been useful, its slow progress through military protocol

in Washington and thence to Fort Shafter was a grim comedy
of bureaucracy in action.

We wondered at the time, when we heard the first part
of the story, why the army would entrust such a critical
message to a civilian communications company.   The
sequence of events came out during the congressional
investigation into the Pearl Harbor attack. Here is the story:

About mid-morning Sunday December 7 in Washington,
an intercepted and decoded message from Japanese Foreign
Minister Shigenori Togo to Ambassador Nomura landed on
several desks in the army, navy and Department of State. It
instructed Nomura to deliver the Japanese rejections of the
U.S.' latest proposal to Secretary of State Hull "at 1 p.m. on
the 7th, your time."   That would have been 7:30 a.m. in
Hawaii, 25 minutes before the Japanese struck.

Nomura requested the appointment as ordered.

Meanwhile, American cryptologists had intercepted and
decoded 13 parts of the 14-part Japanese message. Several
of the mid-level American officers who received the message
to Nomura recognized its importance, but military protocol
prevented their taking immediate direct action on their own.
It was not until after 11 a.m. that it reached General Marshall
and Admiral Harold R. Stark, Chief of Naval Operations, after
they had arrived at their offices.

After some discussion, including a phone conversation
between Marshall and Stark, it was agreed that Marshall
would send a warning message to appropriate army
commands. Stark asked that he include instructions for the
recipients to notify their navy counterparts.

In his own hand, Marshall wrote, "Japanese are presenting
at 1 p.m. Eastern time today what amounts to an ultimatum.
Also they are under orders to destroy their code machines
immediately. Just what significance the hour set may have

we do not know but be on alert accordingly. Inform naval authorities of this communication. Marshall."

At the War Department's Signal Center, there was some delay while Marshall's difficult handwriting was transcribed and coded. Then it was transmitted to commands in the Caribbean, Philippines and the Presidio in San Francisco. The first message went at noon, just 60 minutes before the time for which Nomura had been told to request his meeting with Hull.

Those messages got off all right but atmospheric conditions were creating so much interference on the radio teletype circuit to Hawaii that it could not be used. Consequently, the Signal Center teletyped the message to Western Union for direct relay to RCA in San Francisco for onward relay to Honolulu where RCA had a direct teletype circuit to Fort Shafter.[12]

What the Signal Center officer apparently did not know, however, was that RCA in Honolulu was closed on Sundays and only the Commercial Cable Company was open. Therefore, Western Union had to divert the message to that facility.

By the time the message reached Honolulu, the 1 p.m. (7:30 a.m. Hawaiian time) deadline had passed and the Japanese attack was underway. The one man on duty at the cable company office put the message into an envelope and turned it over to his messenger, probably along with other messages for delivery, and off it went.

On his way, the boy was delayed when he had to take cover during the latter stages of the attack. The message finally reached Fort Shafter late in the morning, long after the last Japanese plane had departed, lay in an "in" basket for awhile, was finally decoded and reached General Short sometime after noon, long after the Japanese attackers had left.

Another warning had to do with a newfangled gadget called "radar". In 1941, radar still was high on the secret list and not many civilians even knew it existed. Correspondents later in the war used to joke that it was so secret that the censors wouldn't let us write about it even if we spelled it backward!

There were a couple of radar stations operating on Oahu on December 7 and a report began to circulate in Honolulu that one of them had reported the approach of the Japanese planes Sunday morning. It was only one of many rumors in a rumor-laden town at the time, but the later investigation revealed that there was substance to it.

Two army enlisted men, Privates George E. Elliott and Joseph L. Lockard, were on duty at the radar site near Kahuku Point on the northern end of Oahu early that morning. They were scheduled to go off duty at 7 a.m. but Elliott, who was new to the assignment, continued to fool with the gadget for a few minutes.

Suddenly, he picked up blips which seemed to indicate a large number of planes approaching from the North. He and Lockard debated whether they should report his, since they were supposed to have closed the station earlier. But they decided to phone it in to the information center at Fort Shafter anyway.

The information center also was supposed to have gone off duty at 7 a.m. but switchboard operator, Private Joseph McDonald, was still there. He answered the call and turned it over to Lieutenant Kermit Tyler. This was only Tyler's second day on the job so he also was inexperienced.

As he came on duty during the night, Tyler had heard that a flight of Flying Fortresses was scheduled to arrive in the morning from San Francisco. After listening to Lockard, Tyler decided that the radar operators had picked up the flight of B-17's, so he dismissed the report and it went no further.

There had been pitifully little aerial resistance to the Japanese Sunday, but a few of our fighters did get into the air despite the lack of warning. Two of them were piloted by a couple of poker-playing young army fliers, Second Lieutenants Kenneth M. Taylor and George S. Welch. Their squadron of P-40 fighters was stationed temporarily at a small field at Haleiwa (ha-lay-ee-va) on Oahu's northwest shore but they had gone to a dance at the Wheeler Field Officers Club Saturday night, then stayed for an all-night poker game. When the firing started at Wheeler at about 8 a.m. Sunday, they ran to Taylor's car and headed for Haleiwa, 10 miles away, spurred on by some Japanese strafing.

At Haleiwa they were dispatched to patrol over Barber's Point where they intercepted a formation of six Japanese planes. In the ensuing dogfight, Taylor and Welch each shot down two Japanese.

They returned to Wheeler for more ammunition for their machine guns. As they helped ground crewmen load the ammunition, the second wave of Japanese attackers swooped down on the field. While ground crews dove for cover, Taylor and Welch took off.

This was one segment of the action in which the Japanese ran into some opposition. There were several other Americans in the air by this time, too. Welch got two more Japanese and the army later cited four more pilots for getting one each.

Second Lieutenant Philip Rasmussen shot down one of them in a dogfight over Schofield Barracks, witnessed by hundreds of spectators on the ground who came out from the hiding places they had found when the attack began. They cheered as the Japanese plane burst into flames and fell.

While few civilians left the designated evacuation areas for refuge farther from the shore, most women and children were evacuated from the military bases Sunday afternoon. The Japanese had bombed and strafed most of them, particularly the air bases, and even at Schofield Barracks, the big infantry base next to Wheeler Field, one witness said "the bombs dropped like hail."

Consequently, women and children were ordered to safer locations, most of which were Honolulu schools and the University of Hawaii. It was late afternoon before some of the busses assigned to move the refugees left the bases. Darkness fell as the drivers tried to find their way through unfamiliar streets in the blackout. At frequent intervals, nervous sentries, their rifles at the ready, barked a challenge. In the distance, anti-aircraft fire boomed and lighted the sky as gunners fired at imaginary attackers. It was no wonder that some of the refugees were near hysteria by the time they reached their destinations.

Late in the day, we learned that we had a new competitor in town. Like UP, the Associated Press was a two-man operation which was run by Hugh Lytle with Eugene Burns as his assistant. Hugh was a captain in the army reserve and had to report to duty immediately after the attack began, leaving Burns to work alone.

Fortunately for Gene, help was at hand although he didn't know it until it walked into his bureau Sunday afternoon. The help was Tom Yarborough, an AP correspondent being transferred to the Middle East, who was on a Dutch ship which he said had "eased into sunny Honolulu harbor at the height of the attack."

Yarborough said he and the other passengers thought they had arrived in the midst of a big scale war game.

"The passengers crowded the decks and applauded the navy for timing it for our arrival," he wrote a few days later. "A bomb hit the water about 100 yards away and a passenger said, "Boy, what if that had been a real one!"

Then an officer, perspiring and with his hands trembling, herded the passengers into a lounge and told them that, indeed, it was the real thing. As they debarked in groups of 20 and sought transportation to their hotels, the passengers saw autos, trucks and fire engines with screaming sirens speeding by. By Monday however they were mingling with Christmas shoppers in the stores and shops and with civilians and guardsmen in the streets.(13)

While our own antiaircraft shells, not Japanese bombs, did most of the damage in Honolulu, damage to some buildings was significant. Most of them were in residential districts where a number of homes were gutted by explosions and fires. The projectile which exploded near Governor Poindexter's residence and killed a man across the street left a crater about five feet in diameter and almost as deep. It was no wonder that people thought they were being bombed.

As Monday afternoon wound down, homebound traffic filled the streets earlier than usual. Everyone wanted to get home before nightfall and blackout time. It would be another nervous night.

25: Baby Bed at Midway

At sea, the *Enterprise* was getting dangerously low on fuel. Halsey had to take the big carrier and her escorts into Pearl Harbor to gas up.

As the task force approached Oahu Monday night, Halsey sent his planes ashore and this time they made it without triggering American anti-aircraft fire.

Eight of Fighting Six's wildcats took off from the carrier's deck at 4:30 p.m. for Wheeler Field and four more followed an hour later. As Jim Gray flew in toward Wheeler, he saw the mess at Pearl Harbor for the first time.

"The *Arizona* was still blazing," he said, "and you know the feeling of seeing all that devastation."

At Wheeler the pilots found the field in bad shape. In its own way, the big Army Air Corps fighter base was as much a mess as Pearl Harbor. Scores of ravaged planes littered the landscape and hangars and other buildings stood gutted by fire, walls and roofs blown out by explosions.

The Fighting Six pilots were ordered to disperse their planes along the concrete apron. There was too much mud to put them into the defense bunkers designed to protect parked planes against aerial attack—bunkers which had not been used for that purpose the previous morning because Wheeler's planes had been bunched for protection against possible sabotage.

The *Enterprise* pilots ate in an emergency mess hall and were billeted in private quarters for the night because the field's regular mess halls and barracks had been destroyed.

"Black as hell, it was," said the diary. "Much machine gun and rifle fire kept the pilots from sleeping during the night."

But before nightfall, Gray had an errand to do. He still had family belongings at the house in Waialea which the Browns had taken over, so he borrowed a jeep for a quick run into Honolulu. Of course, he didn't find Anne and Sam there, but he quickly threw his things into the jeep, including infant Dougie's folding baby bed which wound up with him back on the *Enterprise*.

"It was the only baby bed present at the Battle of Midway, I'm sure," Jim said later.

Back at Wheeler, Gray successfully answered the sentry's challenge which was "George Washington."

"I've often wondered how many guys got shot at when they didn't reply, "Valley Forge," Jim said. Considering the difficulty most Japanese have in the pronunciation of words containing an "l" or an "r", it was a logical password that night.

Meanwhile, the *Enterprise* had moved slowly into the harbor after nightfall, her crew aghast at what they could see of the destruction on Battleship Row. Quickly, the work of refueling and restocking the big ship and her escorts went forward.

A little after 3 a.m., the job was done and by dawn, she was at sea again, ready to pick up her birds which had spent the night ashore and resume the hunt.

26: "Sam's Safe" (Kay)

None of us felt rested when we awoke Tuesday. We hadn't slept well because of that constant worry about our husbands. Although Frank still was in Honolulu, he was a reporter—now a war correspondent—and I knew that sooner or later he would have to go where the action was. That was unless the action came to us first.

The others were even more worried. Their men might already be in action, or worse.

Then the phone rang. It was Howell Forgy, the chaplain on the *New Orleans*, Sam's and Harry Hahn's ship. He was calling as many of the wives as he could reach to tell them that their husbands were safe. Thank God!

I told him I'd get the information to Janet and Anne Brown right away. Howell couldn't say any more because of security.

Poor Sue and Mary. Howell had no information on the *Sothard* and the *Detroit* so they still had no idea what might have happened to Bob and Don or where they were. I called Anne and Janet immediately and they were so relieved.

After breakfast, Sue, Mary and I decided to take a walk, even though it was a drizzly day. Rain seldom bothered us in Hawaii. We really needed to buy some food, but that was impossible today since Governor Poindexter had ordered all food stores closed until tomorrow.

Manoa Valley was a beautiful residential area in the hills behind Honolulu, quiet and peaceful, its homes mostly hidden from the streets by heavy foliage. We looked for signs of bomb damage but found none in this relatively protected valley.

As we strolled along, everyone we met wanted to talk. People always seem to get that way when they've been through a crisis. Many wanted to get out of Hawaii on the first available transportation. The bombing, the rumors, the worry about what might happen next had frightened a lot of people.

Our group was not among them, however. We were frightened, but we wanted to stay as long as we could. The navy wives knew that they would be sent to The States on the first available transportation and there was nothing they could do about it. The big question for them was, "Will I get to see my husband again before I have to leave?"

As for me, I was going to stay, period.

I had a happy surprise late in the afternoon when Frank called to say he would join us for dinner and would spend the night. We all would be glad to have a man in the house again.

While we were at dinner, the phone rang. It was the transpacific operator with a person-to-person call for Frank. This puzzled us because the communications blackout still was on;   no phone calls or messages were permitted to or from The Territory.

When Frank picked up the phone, a censor in San Francisco said he had Frank Bartholomew, vice president and Pacific Division manager of United Press, on that end. He said that Mr. Bartholomew had been given permission to make the call only to ascertain the welfare of the UP staff and that of our clients. The censor said he would listen in, that Frank and Bart should not attempt to discuss anything else, and that they had just three minutes.

Bart was pretty clever. He wasn't going to get any military information, but he was going to get the first story out of Hawaii since Sunday morning. UP's logo would be on the first Honolulu dateline since December 7.

I could hear Frank telling Bart that he, Bill and Mac were all fine as were Beth and Sharon Tyree and I. He said that Lorrin Thurston, publisher, and Ray Coll, Sr., editor of the *Advertiser*, and Joe Farrington, publisher, and Riley Allen, editor of the *Star-Bulletin*, and all their staffs also came through the attack with no casualties, as had the staffs and families of the other Hawaiian clients, and that none of their buildings had been damaged.

Well, it wasn't much of a story but, given the lack of any other news out of Hawaii, it was printed in hundreds of newspapers and broadcast on radio news programs all over the country. When I heard that later, as well as accounts of the broadcasts of my story Sunday, it was the first time I'd ever felt famous.

Bart was able to tell Frank that we had beaten everybody on the story and that UP was very proud of us. By that time the three minutes were up.

After dinner, we made a grocery shopping list because we were out of just about everything, and we thought we had better stock up Wednesday when the stores reopened. We had no idea what would be available, but we thought we should get everything we could. Of course, the stores still would be operating under instructions to serve only their regular customers and only in normal amounts, so we wouldn't be allowed to hoard even if we wanted to—or had the money with which to do it.

As a matter of fact, civilians in Hawaii later were encouraged to hoard. Except for small truck farms in rural Oahu and on the outside islands and the meat produced by the Parker Ranch on the Big Island, all of Hawaii's food was imported. Throughout the war, whenever a ship came in with food, it was moved through the warehouses and on to retailers as quickly as possible so there would be storage space available when another ship came in. Civilians were encouraged to buy as much at a time as they could, storing temporary surpluses in their homes.

We never suffered any serious shortages in Hawaii and we never had food rationing as they did on the mainland, but sometimes we were very short of some items and long on others. That occasionally led to some rather unbalanced meals.

As the war went along, meat was the biggest problem as far as food was concerned. Frank's mother, "Ma T", used to tell me, "A girl's best friend is her butcher." She served the best meat, so I followed her example and always tried to be especially friendly with my butcher.

"Ma T" was right and it paid off in Honolulu. Frequently, when I'd arrive to shop, I'd find the meat cases virtually empty, but I seldom walked away empty handed.

"Hello, Mrs. Tremaine," the butcher would say. "Just a minute—I have your order ready."

Then he'd disappear through the door to the big

refrigerator. When he returned, he'd hand me a wrapped package with my name written on it along with the amount to be paid at the checkout counter. I never knew what I had until I got home and unwrapped the package. It wasn't always the best cut you ever saw, but we rarely went without, and usually it was a lot better than one might expect in a short-supply situation.

But that's getting ahead of the story. I told Frank after dinner that I didn't think we should stay at Janet's any longer, that I wanted to get home. I suggested he let me drive him to work in the morning, then Susie, Mary and I would shop, go home, and then I'd bring the car back to him. I knew the car was needed at the bureau, along with Bill's, in case two of them had to go out on different stories at the same time.

In the morning, after I left Frank at the *Advertiser* Building, I returned to Manoa to pick up Sue and Mary and our belongings. On the way back to Alewa Heights, we stopped at Chun Hoon's, the big Chinese grocery and meat market at Nuuanu Valley where we were well known because we did most of our shopping there.

We found the shelves fairly well stocked with staples but the supply of meat was pretty sparse. My butcher apologized. I told him not to worry, gave him my sweetest smile and took what he had.

After unloading at home, I drove back to the *Advertiser*, left the car for Frank and walked to the corner to catch the bus. As luck would have it, I'd just missed the one that ran to Alewa Heights once an hour, so I had a long wait.

When the bus finally arrived, it must have been soon after ship change, because it was full of male defense workers. Workers, mostly single, had been pouring into Honolulu for months, renting houses and apartments in groups all over town. They all seemed to be on the make for anything in a skirt. If she were young, so much the better. I hadn't had to use that bus very often so it was something new for me. I'd never been so leered at in my life! It was downright frightening, not an experience I wanted to repeat.

Frank got home for dinner early enough so we could eat in daylight, before blackout. Thus began a routine which lasted for months. Because of the big windows in most of the house, the only room we could black out was the bedroom. Sometimes we'd have to eat in there when Frank got home late, as he often did, so I'd have to prepare something I could keep warm or serve cold.

Because of his job, Frank had a pass which permitted him to be out after curfew and to drive in the blackout. Of course, we had to have the car's lights painted over. Headlights were painted black except for a thin blue slit about two inches long and a quarter-inch high, and taillights were also blue.

There weren't many cars on the streets at night but those that were out had to move very carefully because those blue slits threw no light on the road and could only be seen for a short distance. Taillights were even worse and there were a few rear-enders on those blacked out streets.

One night when Frank was at sea on the *Indianapolis,* I invited Judy Kinney, wife of a Stanford classmate of Frank's, to come for dinner and to spend the night. Her husband was at sea, too.

I cooked early, as usual, so we could dine while we could still see what we were eating. By the time we had finished, it was dark, so I carefully carried our dishes to the kitchen, located a corner of the counter near the sink by touch, and left them there in a stack to be washed in the morning.

Judy and I repaired to the bedroom to talk and I tried one of the thin lady's cigars that Judy favored. They made us thirsty, so we decided to have a nightcap before turning in. We felt our way back to the kitchen and, while I got glasses and whiskey, Judy groped her way toward the refrigerator for ice.

Crash. . .!

Immediately I knew that nearly half of my only set of dishes was gone. Judy had brushed against them accidentally in the dark. She was distraught, of course. I told her, in all sincerity, not to worry, that they were not expensive and would be easy to replace. No so, however. I discovered that such items were low on the priority list for scarce shipping space and we'd have to make do with what we had for a long time.

Our funny old iron bed became our sofa and our small, cramped bedroom was the parlor for months. We often had friends in despite the cramped quarters. Sometimes there were three or four on the bed, two or three more on the floor and one in the only chair.

The cigarette smoke would get so thick, it's a wonder we didn't die of smoke poisoning, but we didn't care. We'd gab and argue for hours about the war and how Washington was screwing things up, about politics, about all the things young people argue about.

Nobody got angry, though. There was a lot of togetherness in that little room. Maybe it was the closeness or the tensions and spirit of the time—whatever it was, those nights seemed to encourage friendship. We made some wonderful friends among the Honoluluans and the correspondents and service people who passed through town and congregated with us there.

For almost a year, we lived in those strange conditions. Then one day, I discovered several bolts of navy blue denim in Sears. Hallelujah!

I snapped up yards and yards of it and carried it home triumphantly. It was a tough job on my old portable sewing machine to stitch up all the material I had to use to make blackout curtains for all those big windows and to fit them with hooks, but I did it. I never was so pleased with anything in my life. We felt liberated!

Since supplying the Islands was a problem, there really was no room for anyone who did not contribute to the war effort. I had to get a job.

Luckily, not long after the war began, I learned that the Army Signal Corps needed cryptographers at Fort Shafter. I qualified, but the army was suspicious of me because I was a newsman's wife. A cryptographer handles a lot of classified messages and they were afraid I'd tell Frank something I shouldn't. I finally convinced them that I could keep a secret and they hired me.

I had to keep secrets because we encoded and decoded messages between Hawaiian Department Headquarters, the War Department in Washington and the forward areas about all kinds of interesting things. I saw a lot of stuff that Frank would have given his right arm to know, especially when the Guadalcanal campaign got underway, but my lips were sealed. He never asked me about anything, just complained that I knew more about what was going on than he did. He was right!

I had odd working hours and that led to complications. The Signal Corps office was a 24-hour operation, of course, Pearl Harbor but instead of keeping us cryptographers on one shift for several months at a time, they rotated us every week. When I worked the night shift, an army truck would get me home about 1 a.m. and I'd fall into bed dead tired. Then Frank would get up at 5 a.m. I'd throw some breakfast together for him, then try to get back to sleep.

One morning in my daze, I put water in the coffee pot and oatmeal in the double boiler, then poured the dry coffee over the oatmeal. That woke me! It also told me that I couldn't continue that routine much longer. The constantly shifting work pattern kept me from getting enough sleep. I was losing weight and I was exhausted.

Fortunately, I got a call one day from Betty McDonald, the society editor of the *Star-Bulletin*. She also was a part-time correspondent for the NEA Syndicate and they wanted her to work full time for them. Riley Allen didn't want to stand in her way, but he told her she had to find a replacement.

Because of the publicity I'd gotten for my part in the coverage on December 7, Betty and Riley both assumed that I'd had newspaper experience. When I told Betty I'd never even been inside a newspaper office, she said, "Never mind. They're using so little society news now that this job is a snap. Just don't tell Riley."

Thus began my career as a newswoman. Betty was right. The job was a snap, so much so that I quickly got bored. To make life more interesting, I started to write a column and do some other things around the paper and that led to an offer from the rival *Advertiser*.

I told Riley that I wanted to be a general assignment reporter, the job Ray Coll was offering me at the *Advertiser*, and that I couldn't stand that so-called society stuff any longer. Riley wouldn't budge, so I went to the *Advertiser*. That made Riley angry at both me and Frank, much to Frank's dismay, but it was a good move for me because at the *Advertiser* I was able to cover all kinds of stories, including some related to the war. It made me feel much more a part of things, especially when Frank was away in the South Pacific or at CinCPac headquarters after Admiral Nimitz moved to Guam.

Also, Riley didn't stay angry. Both he and Ray were wonderful men and I loved them both. They were among our best friends.

27 : Sabotage?

Rumors of espionage and sabotage by Japanese in Hawaii were fascinating and persistent in the days immediately after the attack. They ranged from the impossible and absurd, such as arrows in the canefields, to the plausible but false, such as contamination of the drinking water.

There also were rumors of bloody retaliation such as one that was current on the cruiser *Indianapolis* when I was with her at sea a month later. According to that story, sailors and Marines still on weekend liberty in Honolulu Sunday night pulled Japanese out of their cars and beat them to death in the streets of Honolulu.

The fact that any sailor or Marine absent from his post Sunday night would have been court martialed and that only a handful of official cars were on the blacked out streets of Honolulu that night never seemed to occur to the rumor mongers.

Even Secretary of Navy Knox fell for some of the reports when he made a flying visit to Pearl Harbor December 11-15. Back in Washington at a press conference on the

16th Knox said, "With the exception of Norway, the most effective fifth-column work in this war was done in Hawaii."

He declined to elaborate but later in the conference, in response to a question, he said, "The net result of it was that pretty complete information had been given to the Japanese. They had almost perfect information about the defenses of the island, the disposition of the fleet and everything else."

Knox was right about that, but the information came from master spy Yoshikawa in the Japanese consulate, not from the American-Japanese of Hawaii.

But much of that is hindsight. As far as Bill, Mac and I were concerned on December 6, Japanese espionage and sabotage was a story we had to check out.

After dismissing the absurdities, it didn't take long to determine that none of the other reported acts of sabotage had taken place either. The most plausible, it seemed to us, was the possibility that enemy agents or sympathizers had contaminated the water supply, but the water company's prompt testing eliminated that one.

But espionage was something else. It seemed obvious that the Japanese pilots were guided by quite precise information. Charts found in some of the downed enemy planes showed routes and targets in accurate detail including ship locations. How did they get it?

We knew nothing of Yoshikawa then. We believed that such information must have come from enemy agents among the population, possibly including some of those grocers and household servants who so often were the subject of cocktail party gossip.

By Monday morning, December 8, there were reports that the FBI and military had picked up a lot of enemy agents. The rumors fed on each other but there was no official information until the army announced later Monday without

Sabotage?

elaboration that "a number of enemy agents and sympathizers have been taken into custody."

Beyond that, official sources were silent but we soon learned that several hundred Japanese had been arrested Sunday and Monday, questioned, held and then, after several days, taken to Sand Island, an unused old immigration station in Honolulu harbor, where they still were. That was more grist for the rumor mill.

In the territory's total population of about 420,000, approximately 156,000 were Japanese of whom about 37,500 were aliens born in Japan (*i-ssei*). The *issei* were ineligible to become naturalized American citizens, but their children born in Hawaii (*nisei*) were citizens by birth. An overwhelming majority of them were proud to be called Americans or even American-Japanese.

Comprising about 37% of the population, the Japanese were engaged in almost every facet of the territory's life. It was natural that the military and FBI would worry about the loyalty of at least some of them, about their potential for espionage and sabotage.

Yet the Japanese, especially the *nisei*, made up a significant portion of the work force. On the one hand, they were needed to make the territory operate. On the other, they were too large a segment of the population to take into custody and pack off to internment camps as was done a few months later with Japanese aliens and American-Japanese in the Pacific Coast states.

Admiral Kimmel and General Short recognized this. They made several speeches in the months preceding the war, lauding and encouraging the loyalty of Hawaiian Japanese. Short's policy was to encourage loyalty of the Japanese population of Hawaii by a promise of fair treatment.

"Success of the campaign would promote unity and

149

greatly reduce the proportions of our defense problem," he told the War Department.

In September 1941, he promised that in the event of war, Japanese aliens legally residing in Hawaii would be protected and that there would be no concentration camps.

Opinion in the haole community about the loyalty of the Hawaiian Japanese was divided. Many, especially among the relative newcomers, were deeply suspicious of them but business and government leaders encouraged Kimmel and Short in promoting Japanese loyalty.

While leaders of the Japanese community sought to promote loyalty to the U.S. in fact and in perception by organizing first-aid classes and other patriotic projects, many Japanese clung to a life style that fostered suspicion. Many Japanese families insisted that their children attend Japanese language schools at the end of the regular school day and it was a commonly held belief that loyalty to Japan, not the U.S., was part of the curriculum.

The fact that the military leaders sought to encourage and promote American Japanese loyalty did not mean that they were not deeply concerned about possible espionage and sabotage. They were.

Army and navy intelligence and the FBI organized an intensive counter-espionage campaign. In January 1941, the Honolulu Police Department joined the effort when Police Chief William A. Gabrielson announced that a new espionage bureau of one lieutenant and four officers would work with the other agencies.

Robert Shivers, the local FBI chief, was particularly concerned about the large number of Japanese consular agents in the Islands, more than 200 of them, who were called *toritsuginin*. These men were mostly elderly *issei* appointed by the Japanese Consul General in the early days of Japanese immigration to Hawaii when thousands of laborers were brought in to work on the sugar and pineapple plantations.

They were respected elders whose job it was to help uneducated, frequently illiterate fellow Japanese deal with legal paper work relating to their immigration status and other personal affairs. They were not paid for their work, but they played an important role in the Japanese community.

Later, as the need for this sort of assistance declined, most of the *toritsuginin* resigned or simply became inactive, but they were suspect in the eyes of the FBI and military intelligence.

Shivers' staff compiled a list of the consular agents and other Island Japanese who were considered to be potentially dangerous. These included owners and crews of the boats of the Japanese sampan fleet, fishing vessels based mostly in Kewalo Basin, a small harbor between downtown Honolulu and Waikiki and only about 12 miles from Pearl Harbor. Their comings and goings from the basin to their fishing grounds, both inshore and well out to sea, put them in a position to observe the movements of Kimmel's fleet.

The navy worried about that and about the possibility that a sampan might sink itself in the narrow entrance to Pearl Harbor, bottling up the fleet until it could be removed.

While the restrictions of diplomacy and law limited the intelligence agencies in their peacetime counter-espionage activities, they moved quickly after the December 7 attack. By afternoon and well into the night, there were knocks on the doors of certain pre-selected Japanese homes.

In his book, *Hawaii—End of the Rainbow*, Kazuo Miyamoto, a *nisei* doctor in Hawaii, describes a typical arrest:

"At the door there were two uniformed men from the

police department or the army. They politely identified themselves, asked for the man they wanted and told him they wanted to take him to police headquarters for 'a few questions.'

"They said the suspect would be detained for only a few hours.

"Outside, the two men escorted their prisoner to a waiting car with another uniformed man behind the wheel. At curbside, the two escorts asked their prisoner to raise his hands, they snapped on handcuffs, then placed him between them in the back seat. To the unsuspecting detainee, this was a shocking development.

"Downtown, instead of going to police headquarters, the car pulled up at the immigration station near the waterfront. Inside, the arresting officers led the prisoner into a room where six army enlisted men were processing arrivals. An officer removed the handcuffs then led the prisoner to a desk where one of the escorts laid down a blue card bearing the man's name. The man behind the desk checked the name against a list which filled several typewritten pages.

"Then the prisoner was instructed to face a wall, put his hands above his head and keep them against the wall. A guard removed the prisoner's belongings from his pockets, placed them in a large envelope bearing the prisoner's name, then told him to climb a dark stairway to the second floor.

"'Another prisoner,' the guard yelled up the stairway.

"On the second floor, he was pushed through a door into a large dark room equipped with three tiers of iron bunks. As the night went on and more prisoners arrived, the room became hot, stuffy and smelly with the odor of human bodies.

"Many of the prisoners knew each other, of course, and there was much discussion of their plight and the day's events.

"On Tuesday (December 9), the prisoners, who included about 20 Germans and Italians, were transferred in small groups to Sand Island, a small chunk of land across Honolulu harbor from the city. It once had been used by the immigration service as a holding station for alien arrivals. It now was manned by a small army detachment whose commanding officer, a captain, told the detainees that they were prisoners of war. Facilities on the island were limited and the men were put to work immediately, erecting tents for their own shelter.

"It was a cold day—for Hawaii—with a drizzling rain. There were no cots that night and the two blankets handed to each prisoner did little to protect the mostly old men—in their 50's to 80's—from the wet ground. Later, canvas cots were brought in but mattresses were supplied only to those sick enough to be sent to the hospital tent.

" As prisoners of war, the men were held incommunicado and denied anything which might be turned into a weapon or tool such as razors, mirrors and other such personal items.

"Because the prisoner's families heard nothing from them after they disappeared into the silence of their military detention, unsettling rumors about their fate spread, particularly in the Japanese community. When news people inquired, officials would say nothing.

This changed, however, after a visit to the camp by Lieutenant General Delos Emmons, who had replaced Short as commander of the Hawaiian Department. He promptly reversed earlier orders and on December 20, the prisoners' status was changed to that of 'detained aliens.' Thereafter they were allowed to communicate with their families and to have basic personal supplies."(14)

But official suspicion persisted. On December 22, the

War Department announced in Washington that 273 "fifth columnists" had been arrested among the Japanese nationals in Hawaii. The announcement said that "for the most part," there was no evidence of disloyalty among the Japanese but some had "provided the enemy with valuable information". Military authorities "have imprisoned all known Japanese leaders of subversive activities. . .and are continuing to search out dangerous individuals," the announcement said.

In Honolulu, however, in a radio broadcast General Emmons said there had been "very few cases of actual sabotage." He said that both the authorities and the public must be alert, but recognizing the important role of the Hawaiian Japanese, he added, "We cannot afford unnecessarily and indiscriminately to keep any. . .loyal workers from useful employment." He suggested that if an employer doubted the loyalty of any worker he would check with the authorities before taking any action. Believing and repeating rumors was playing into enemy hands, he said, and he warned against it. As for the aliens detained on Sand Island, he said they "are not prisoners of war and will not be treated as such."

In January, boards consisting of two civilians and one military officer began questioning each detainee in individual hearings. Generally, the questions had to do with the detainee's work as a consular agent, his support for either government. In most cases, there was only one hearing, although a few detainees were called back for more questioning at considerable length.(15)

On February 14, the army announced that "several rumored enemy aliens who have been interned since December 7 would be sent to the mainland soon." The army said these aliens were not prisoners of war nor criminals but that they had been interned for their own safety. Under

154

international law, aliens could not be interned in combat zones.

No word of this reached Sand Island until two days later when 20 Germans and Italians and 180 of the Japanese suddenly were told to pack their belongings, that they would not return to the island. While the internees had not been warned of the impending move, their families had, so they had packed warm clothing and other essentials for the men to take with them. The army permitted no family meetings before the internees were shipped out on an army transport February 20, bound for San Francisco. From the West Coast, they went by train to Sparta, Wisconsin, for internment there and elsewhere for the duration of the war.(16)

Meanwhile in Hawaii, Japanese and American-Japanese, *issei* and *nisei*, lived in a difficult situation. Unlike the mainland West Coast, there was no internment in Hawaii and they lived and worked without restriction. Yet they were under a cloud of suspicion which impelled many of them to go to extra effort to prove their loyalty. In most cases, the effort was sincere and involved personal sacrifice, but none was greater than the thousands who volunteered for military service.

Many already were in service when the War Department, in January, 1943, called for 1,500 American-Japanese volunteers from Hawaii. Within a month, the volunteers totaled 9,507.

Most of the Hawaiian-Japanese served with the 100th Infantry Battalion and 442nd Regimental Combat Team in some of the bloodiest fighting of the campaign in Italy and later in France. In 10 months in Italy, the 1300-man 100th Battalion had more than 300 killed and 650 wounded. The battalion and combat team together won more than 1,150 medals of various kinds, not counting purple hearts, and 132 commendations.

For several reasons including possible mistaken identity in combat, few American-Japanese served in the Pacific but some did, mostly as interpreters, and most served with distinction.

The attack on Pearl Harbor was a sneak punch but Hawaiian-Japanese did not help deliver it.

28 : More Caskets Than Mourners

Tuesday, December 9—there were a number of funerals in Honolulu today. The caskets outnumbered the mourners.

Actually, the first took place Monday evening and they continued for several days. In a UP dispatch dated December 14, I wrote:

"A grim reminder of the Japanese treachery on December 7 is the row on row of fresh graves covered with tropical greenery in Nuuanu Cemetery on the outskirts of Honolulu where navy victims of the Pearl Harbor attack lie buried.

"Brief military services for the dead began Monday night at Nuuanu and other cemeteries. With the exception of the naval chaplains who conducted the services and a few naval men, they were unattended.

"Each man was buried in an individual coffin, seven coffins to a trench. The raw earth was covered with floral decorations peculiar to this outpost of the United States in the defense of which these men died. Multicolored tropical flowers were worked into backgrounds of green banyan leaves, ti leaves and ferns.

"One row of graves had a 10-foot V for victory' made of white anthuriums. Others were decorated with bird of paradise, torch ginger, red ginger, gladioli, cup of gold, orchids and hibiscus. Many had red, white and blue decorations. Each grave is identified and will be marked later with a headstone."

29: The Damage -- Closeup

On December 7, the *President Coolidge*, an American President Lines passenger ship, was in Far Eastern waters, having just left Shanghai for Manila, Honolulu and San Francisco.

When news of Pearl Harbor and the Japanese attacks on the Philippines, Guam, Wake and other targets reached her captain, he set a course far away from normal shipping lanes where Japanese submarines might be prowling. He took her deep into the South Pacific, giving a wide berth to any islands from which he might be intercepted by a Japanese force.

Finally, his circuitous route brought the *Coolidge* into Honolulu Harbor about 10 days after the war began, putting at rest fears that she might have been captured by the Japanese navy or torpedoed by one of its submarines.

Among the passengers on the *Coolidge* was Wallace Carroll, manager of the United Press bureau in London and, in post-war years, editor and publisher of the Raleigh, North Carolina *News & Observer*. After 15 months of directing UP coverage of the war in Europe and living through the London blitz, Carroll was taking the long way home for a well-deserved vacation from war.

We had known that Carroll was on the *Coolidge* and were fearful that he had been lost, so when he called from dockside as soon as the ship tied up, it was a great relief. When he arrived at the bureau we discussed how we might use his presence and his well known by-line to UP's benefit.

I called Lieutenant Commander Waldo Drake, the chief CinCPac Public Relations Officer, to tell him that Carroll was with us and that I would like to bring him out to Pearl Harbor. Drake invited us to come the next day, which was alright since the *Coolidge* would be in port for two days.

When we arrived at the Pearl Harbor gate the next afternoon, the sentry made a telephone check, then directed us to the CinCPac Headquarters at the Submarine Base. When we reached Drake's desk, located in the center of a large room on the second floor, overcrowded with desks and bustling with the activity of scores of officers and enlisted men, we were surprised at what he had arranged for us. Up to now, the navy had been exceedingly close-mouthed about the success of the Japanese attack. It had admitted nothing beyond the official announcement of December 8 and Knox's December 16 press conference.

"Come on," said Drake, "We're going to take a boat ride."

Downstairs we went and out to a nearby slip where a launch manned by two sailors awaited us. Drake, Carroll and I stepped aboard and the launch pulled away.

From the vicinity of the slip, our view toward the main channel and beyond to Ford Island was obstructed by buildings on both sides of the passage. As we approached the channel, or East Loch, the south end of Ford Island lay dead ahead.

Then as our bow began to swing to starboard, the *California* came into view. The bow swung a little more and there lay the rest of battleship row!

I had some idea of what to expect, but I was shocked. Carroll was aghast. To think that these supposedly invincible battleships, the pride of the American fleet, could have been so devastated in less that two hours. To think of the hundreds of men who had died in the explosions and fires that wracked those great ships in a sneaky Sunday morning attack.

The *California*, moored at the south end of the row along the shore of the island, had taken two torpedo hits early in the attack, then bombs. She rested on the muddy bottom, listing in the shallow water, down by the bow. Scarred by the bombs and blackened here and there by fire, she certainly would have sunk had the water been deeper.

Then came the *Oklahoma* and *Maryland* abreast. The *Oklahoma*, on the outboard side, had taken the heaviest hits and was capsized, her bare bottom protruding above the water.

The *Maryland*, on the inboard side, showed the effects of fires but did not seem to be badly damaged.

Next came the *Tennessee*, inboard, and the *West Virginia*. Again, the inboard ship did not seem to be badly hit but a torpedo had torn a huge hole in the side of the *West Virginia*. She was listing and showed the effects of fire and bomb hits in addition to the torpedo damage. Like the *California*, her bottom rested in the shallow mud which had prevented her from foundering.

Then came what was left of the *Arizona*, wracked by torpedoes and bombs. Early in the attack, a torpedo had passed beneath the repair ship *Vestal*, then moored outboard of the battleship, and smashed into the *Arizona* below the waterline. She had taken repeated bomb hits and, while the story that one had gone down her smokestack probably was not true, a bomb or torpedo had detonated her forward

161

magazine. She lay there now, her bow gone, her forward mast tipped drunkenly forward, her decks awash. The explosion had killed more that 1,000 men including Rear Admiral Isaac C. Kidd, Commander Battleship Division One, and the skipper, Captain Franklin van Valkenburg.

We passed around the north end of Ford Island and came down its west side. There lay the old battleship *Utah*, relegated to target ship duty. Like the *Oklahoma*, she too was bottom up. The Japanese thought they had gotten the aircraft carrier *Lexington* because that was where she was berthed before she left for Midway Island Friday morning.

As we came around the south end of Ford Island, we could see the wrecked hangars of Patrol Wing One and some of the rest of the devastation on the island.

To our right, on the other side of the channel, the *Nevada* lay ahead of us, aground on a sandy point on the west side of the harbor entrance. Her story, we learned later, was one of the most dramatic of a day of dramatic events: On the morning of the 7th, she had been moored at the north end of Battleship Row just beyond the *Arizona* and *Vestal*, and she took some of the first Japanese bombs. One tore a huge hole in her port bow and others started fires which raged through the vessel.

Across the harbor on the hospital ship *Solace,* one of the Nevada's officers, Lieutenant Lawrence Ruff, saw what was happening to his ship.

"I saw a flight of planes flying toward Battleship Row dropping torpedoes," he said in a statement released later by the navy. "I even saw one headed for my ship but the plane burst into flames and a loud cheer went up."

Ruff ordered a launch to take him to the *Nevada*.

"I was stunned by the horribleness of the thing," Ruff continued. "The air was literally filled with planes. I couldn't understand why many raiders didn't come down in that blaze of fire from our ships but the scoundrels stayed right on their course.

"I went through a strafing attack as I approached the ship but got under cover of the starboard gangway, then went up to seek my battle station.   All guns were going and all defenses were manned. I ducked under the lee side of the signal bridge and finally got into the conning tower."

The *Nevada's* skipper was ashore and Lieutenant Commander J.F. Thomas, the senior officer aboard, was at his normal battle station below deck. Ruff was the senior officer on deck.

"Then I saw a torpedo hit the battleship *Arizona*, which was near by—it was a dead sound like a big swish of wind going through foliage," Ruff said. "Another bomb went down the *Arizona's* stack."

Whether the bomb actually went down the stack and reached the ship's forward magazine or whether it was the torpedo, one caused the explosion which blew off the *Arizona's* bow and sent her up in flames.

"I believed the flames would reach the bow of our ship and suggested that we get under way," Ruff went on. "The engine room said it would take half an hour, but I said we had better get under way right now."

Her crew accomplished the job in 10 minutes or less.

"We cast off the lines, backed the engines and started moving out," Ruff said. "We cleared the *Arizona* and a repair ship [*Vestal*] which was alongside by about 40 feet. Our gun crews shielded the ammunition with their own bodies as we moved past the blazing *Arizona*."

With machine guns and antiaircraft guns blazing, she headed for the narrow harbor entrance, past her burning sister ships along Battleship Row, seeking escape to the open

163

sea.

Suddenly, she became a primary target. If the Japanese could sink her in the narrow entrance, she would plug it for days, preventing other ships from entering or leaving, immobilizing the fleet.

"As we squared off down the channel, the Japanese began dive-bombing," Ruff continued. "The ship was hit several times and shivered and shook while our batteries took the Japanese under fire."(17)

A bomb hit amidship, then another on the bridge. She took two or three torpedo hits and began listing to port.

Seaman 1c Lee Miller had been sent below for gas masks because of spreading fumes. "When I returned. . .the whole bridge was aflame," he said. "There was someone helping a wounded officer. We had to help him down by going over the side to the boat deck because the ladder was so hot he could not step on it."(18)

In fact, the Nevada was so seriously damaged that she was in danger of sinking right where the Japanese wanted her to, so Thomas ordered her run aground on Hospital Point on the east side of the channel. Later in the morning, a tug towed her across to the western side of the channel where she lay now, her starboard bow aground on a sandy point.

"I saw acts of heroism that I'll never forget," Ruff said. "I saw a Marine second lieutenant pull a piece of shrapnel out of another Marine's back and this Marine continued to work his machine gun throughout the attack."(19)

As our launch left the Nevada behind and proceeded north up the channel again, we passed the floating drydock where lay the destroyer Shaw, her bow blown off. (Before the war ended, she had been towed to the West Coast, her bow replaced and she returned to action.)

In the next drydock was the battleship Pennsylvania.

The Damage--Closeup

Despite a direct bomb hit, she seemed to have suffered little damage.   Ahead of her in the drydock, however, the destroyers *Cassin* and *Downes* were total wrecks.

The fate of the *Pennsylvania* might have been different had she been in her usual berth at Dock 1010 (called "Ten-ten"). Instead, the ancient minelayer *Oglala,* once a Fall River Line boat, had taken her place. Now she and the cruiser *Helena* inboard of her came into view, both heavily damaged. Later the *Oglala* was listed as lost but the *Helena* was repaired and returned to the war.

Back at the Sub Base, when we stepped off the launch I thanked Waldo for giving us such an extraordinary view of the condition of the fleet. I didn't think it politic just then to ask why he had done it but I couldn't understand it, grateful as I was.

Except for employees of the yard, Wally and I may have been the first civilians to have seen the wreckage. Why? It was not in keeping with the navy's normal reticence about information, especially information which was potentially so damaging, both militarily and politically.

In my case, of course, I was subject to strict censorship and could not write about what we had seen, even had I wanted to jeopardize the navy's security, which I did not. But Wally was sailing the next day for home where he would not be subject to such direct restriction. While the press in the States conformed to strict guidelines of what could be printed it was relatively free compared with the war zones. Wally would not have violated the trust any more than I would but Waldo didn't know him.

While Wally would not write about the extent of the damage he had seen, he could report it verbally to our top people such as Hugh Baillie, president of UP; Earl Johnson, the editor, and Lyle Wilson, our Washington manager, so I could take comfort now in the fact that my headquarters would know exactly what the situation was.

That knowledge would guide them in handling UP's reportage, in evaluating the claims of enemy propaganda as well as the statements of some American sources with big mouths and little information.

I've never forgotten that scene in Pearl Harbor. The memory of the bare-bottomed *Oklahoma*, the wreckage of the *Arizona* is indelible. The thought of the men who died there was with me throughout the war and especially in Tokyo Bay on September 2, 1945.

Epilogue - Surrender on the Missouri

It's another Sunday morning, September 2, 1945, three long years, eight months and 25 days since Japan sucker-punched us at Pearl Harbor. It seems like a lifetime since December 7, 1941. For millions of men and women, and children, too, it was the end of a lifetime.

I'm perched on a forward 16-inch gun turret on the battleship *Missouri*, my feet dangling over the edge. We're anchored in Tokyo Bay, 35 miles south of the city, 4,000 bloody miles west of Hawaii and about six miles offshore from Yokosuka, the Japanese naval base where our Marines landed only three days ago. We're surrounded by scores of ships of the United States Third Fleet and British Pacific Fleet. Many of them, like the 45,000-ton *Missouri*, have been built in the comparatively brief time since the Japanese thought they had knocked us out at Pearl Harbor.

Overhead, planes patrol, some of them from the fleet's carriers, out of sight at sea but maintaining a careful watch even at this time of surrender.

Clouds hang low over the Miura Peninsula to the west, hiding Mt. Fujiyama, the traditional symbol of Japan, as though to shroud it from this scene of national shame.

In my mind's eye, there is another shameful scene. I still

167

see the battered ships on Battleship Row in Pearl Harbor, the *Arizona* twisted and broken where 1,000 men died in an instant, the *Oklahoma* bottom up, five others saved from sinking only by the shallow bottom on which they rest. I recall the mourning for the 3,303 men and women killed or missing in Japan's sneak attack.

It's a far different scene here this morning. Flags fly gaily from every ship, crews are dressed in their whites. On the *Missouri* the flags of all the Allied powers flutter in the breeze

There is a sense of celebration here, of great happiness that at last this war is over and we've won, but it is not the spontaneous hat-throwing, hugging-and-kissing sort of celebration that exploded on VE and VJ days. The mood here today is different. It's reflected in smiles, laughter, some gloating, yet there is a feeling of seriousness, too. There is weighty business at hand.

A chaplain leads the ship in a prayer of thanksgiving. At 8 a.m., the ship's band plays the "Star Spangled Banner" while a detail raises the American flag, the same one which flew over The Capitol in Washington on the "Day of Infamy" in 1941. The *Missouri's* mighty 16-inch guns point to the sky, elevated to 45 degrees.

Sailors in fresh whites and Marines in pressed suntans crowd the *Missouri's* decks and hang from every vantage point on her superstructure. Scattered among them are 238 correspondents including Bill Tyree and Web Edwards, the announcer who told Hawaii to "Take cover. This is an air raid. This is no drill." He is here for CBS.

Francis McCarthy, who was born in the Philippines, is not here, however. He went into Manila with American troops to liberate prisoners of war from the Japanese at Santo Tomas prison, searched out members of his own family who had been held there throughout the war, and now is with them back in the States.

Sam Brown, now a full commander, is down at Saipan in the Marianas Islands south of us in command of a new navy air group. He and his planes and airmen will be assigned to the *Intrepid,* a new carrier. Like many of the rest of us, he would be preparing for his part in what probably would have been a bloody invasion of Japan if peace had not come.

Jim Gray, also a commander now after spending most of the war on the *Enterprise* and leading the navy's first carrier-borne night fighter group, is at the Naval Academy in Annapolis. He is aide to its new Superintendent, Vice Admiral Aubrey (Jake) Fitch who commanded Allied aircraft in the South Pacific campaign.

Harry Albright, now a lieutenant colonel, is assistant G-2 at the Presidio in San Francisco.

Kay, now a reporter and columnist on the *Advertiser*, is at home in Honolulu with our 21-month-old daughter, Nancy. Among other things, this is our sixth wedding anniversary.

Crowded on the gun turret with me are a couple of dozen other correspondents, mostly American but some Australians and British, too.

About 20 feet below us, some one hundred high-ranking American and other Allied officers mill about on the verandah deck where the ceremony soon will begin.

The verandah deck is a small area forward and starboard of the bridge high above us. It is a few feet above the starboard main deck and open to the sea on that side. Our gun turret is its inboard wall.

This is Fleet Admiral William F. Halsey's flagship and, at the aft end of the deck a door leads to his quarters. Beside the door, hanging on the bulkhead, is a picture frame encasing the flag Commodore Matthew Perry flew when he sailed into Tokyo Bay in 1853 to open Japan to American ships. It is frayed and tattered but its 31 stars are clearly visible.

The deck is about 40 feet wide at that end. About halfway down the starboard side, open to the sea, it narrows toward a short flight of steps leading to the main deck below.

Beneath my dangling feet, Halsey and Vice Admiral Jock McCain, the fast carrier task force commander, are chatting happily. It was Halsey who had said early in the war that he was going to ride Emperor Hirohito's white horse down the Ginza in Tokyo. That was late in 1942 when the Guadalcanal campaign was going so badly and he said it to buck up his flagging troops.

Now he's just happy to be here, horse or no horse. Suddenly, McCain breaks into a little dance step, almost a jig. Then he grabs Halsey by the arm. I can't hear what they're saying but they grin like a couple of kids just out of school. [Four days later, McCain died of a heart attack.]

At 8:05 a.m., Fleet Admiral Chester W. Nimitz, Commander-in-Chief Pacific and Pacific Ocean Areas (CinCPac-CinCPOA), is piped aboard. It was he who flew from Washington to Pearl in December 1941 to take command of the shattered fleet, taking over in a brief ceremony the day after Christmas under a dark and gloomy sky on the deck of a submarine berthed near his headquarters building.

Less than six months later that fleet, still only a shadow of what it was to become, wrecked a Japanese armada at Midway, the turning point of the war in the Pacific.

Then General Douglas MacArthur's forces in the Southwest Pacific stopped the Japanese in New Guinea while Nimitz, with Halsey in command on the scene, took Guadalcanal away from them in the Solomons.

The Battle of Midway was fought June 4-6, 1942. We

landed on Guadalcanal in August and Japanese resistance ended there February 9, 1943 after some of the bitterest fighting of the war.

In an interview in Tokyo a few weeks after the surrender, Admiral Mitsumasa Yonai, the Japanese navy minister and a former prime minister, would tell me that knowledgeable Japanese military men knew they would not win the war after they lost Guadalcanal.

Yet they fought tenaciously for another two and a half years at a cost of millions of dead and wounded in their armed forces and civilian population and tens of thousands of Allied casualties.

It was not until August 15, 1945, after our atomic bombs obliterated Hiroshima and Nagasaki, that Emperor Hirohito told his people in a brief radio speech, "We have decided to effect a settlement of the present situation by resorting to an extraordinary measure. . . ."

The extraordinary measure was Japan's acceptance of the Allies' demand for unconditional surrender.

On Guam, where Nimitz had his headquarters, five assault transports were loaded quickly with the reactivated Fourth Marine Regiment. They were the old "China Marines" who had served in China for many years and had been wiped out in the Philippines at Corregidor at the start of the war. So great was the hurry that the Marines and their equipment, with a handful of us correspondents, were loaded in 22 hours. Normally the job would have taken four days.

Our transports left Guam on August 12 and rendezvoused with Halsey's Third Fleet August 19. In the Philippines Army units prepared for aerial transport to Japan.

It was a case of hurry up and wait. Our fleet of approximately 150 ships cruised slowly back and forth, back and forth 200 to 300 miles off the southern Japanese island

171

of Kyushu. We couldn't see them all, of course, because they were spread out over hundreds of square miles but there were aircraft carriers, battleships, cruisers, destroyers, mine sweepers, transports, supply and fuel vessels, all with no place t go while the millstones of military diplomacy ground slowly at MacArthur's headquarters in Manila. American and Japanese representatives were discussing procedure.

Finally, *The Word*. The Marines would land August 30 at Yokosuka, the naval base 35 miles south of Tokyo, while elements of the Army's 11th Airborne and 27th Divisions landed at Atsugi air field, also south of the capitol.

The initial landing forces numbered no more than 15,000 men. They were outnumbered by the Japanese Home Army of a million men or more, but they were supported by hundreds of aircraft and the guns of the Third Fleet, and not a shot was fired. They landed in a nation which had been invaded only three times in its history, never successfully, one which still had intact an army of approximately 3,000,000 men.

"Probably no greater gamble has been taken in history," MacArthur said two weeks later.

At Yokosuka, Vice Admiral Oscar C. Badger took the surrender of the base from a scruffy-looking group of Japanese naval officers and a few spit-and-polish officers of the Home Army. The army had hoped to greet the first Americans in Japan in a far more belligerent fashion under much different circumstances. Only the Emperor's decision to surrender prevented the bloody greeting they had planned for an Allied invasion.

Our troops quickly secured the air field and naval base and set up a defense line across the peninsula. The schedule called for them to move slowly until major reinforcements arrived. Tokyo was not to be occupied until the following week, six days after the surrender. It was off-limits until then.

But that didn't keep the correspondents out. On one expedition into the city, we found a sign which told us that some of the population, at least, was preparing a friendly welcome. It stood in a store window and advertised, "King Anne Scotch—Genuine Scotch-type Scotch."

On the afternoon of September 1, Captain Harold E. Stassen, Halsey's assistant chief of staff, invited me to accompany him and a navy team on a rescue mission to a civilian internment camp on the far side of Tokyo. In 1938 Stassen had been elected governor of Minnesota at the age of 31, the youngest state governor in history. After the war, he was a frequent, unsuccessful candidate for the Republican nomination for President.

We sailed up Tokyo Bay in the USS *Reeves*, a destroyer-sized troop transport, and tied up at a dock on the south waterfront. We were farther into the inner harbor of Tokyo Bay than any Allied vessel yet had ventured. Two commandeered Japanese trucks with U.S. navy drivers awaited us.

At first, as our party of about 50 bluejackets and officers set out on our 75-mile journey, we saw little damage. Then we came to a devastated area about a mile square. Beyond that in the downtown business district, many modern buildings seemed to be mostly intact, others showed some bomb damage and a few had been destroyed.

The Emperor's palace, glimpsed through the trees of the park which surrounded it, appeared undamaged, but such was not the case. It had suffered some damage and the Emperor actually was living in a cottage on the palace grounds.

But then came block after block of burned-out areas. In reporting on the B-29s' incendiary raids on Tokyo in March,

I had quoted an air force statement which had said that an area approximately the size of Manhattan Island had burned in one night. Here was the evidence. Later estimates said that between 80,000 and 130,000 people had died in that huge attack on March 9, as many or more than were killed by the atomic bomb at Hiroshima.

As far as we could see, only a few brick or concrete structures still stood and those were mostly gutted. People were living in hundreds of crude shacks that dotted the ash-strewn, debris-covered landscape, most built of salvaged corrugated metal or other scrap. From time to time, we saw a chimney still erect, a small safe standing on a concrete slab, some wrecked lathes and other light machinery, mute evidence that small industry had operated here. Truly, it was the world's biggest ash heap.

A few days earlier, a Japanese radio broadcast had said that nearly ten million Japanese had been killed, wounded or left homeless by the war. It said that 44 cities had been almost completely wiped out and that in 37 other cities, at least one-third of the industrialized areas had been gutted. I could believe it now.

Occasionally, we passed a coughing, charcoal-burning automobile. There were a few street cars and electric interurbans and a number of bicycle riders. Curious stares greeted our two truckloads of khaki-clad Americans but only occasionally did we see any sign of hostility. In the suburbs we began to see a few smiles from children.

When we stopped briefly to ask directions, curious youngsters shyly smiled and waved while their elders stood back, aloof. But when we resumed our journey they also waved good-bye.

At our destination, a Franciscan monastery in the suburb of Urawa, we found 56 civilian male internees of various

Epilogue

Western nationalities. Most of them seemed to be in pretty good physical condition but a few needed medical attention so we took them back with us. None showed the signs of hunger and mistreatment that had been found among those of our prisoners of war who already had been rescued from Japanese POW camps.

The trip back to the waterfront was completed in darkness. Tokyo no longer was blacked out but it might as well have been. There were no street lights and only dim lights glowed in the windows of a few of the ramshackle shacks. Most of them in the bombed out areas were without lights. Although we had seen a few street cars on the way out, there was a serious power shortage.

Back on the *Missouri* on Sunday morning, it's 8:15 now and the foreign delegations begin to arrive—the Chinese, Australians, Canadians, French, Dutch, New Zealanders and the Soviets, who got in just under the wire by declaring war on Japan on August 9, the day we dropped the second atomic bomb on Nagasaki. They are in full uniform complete with decorations. Then came the British. In keeping with their American hosts, they wear white shorts and shirts, open at the throat, and no decorations.

All the American officers are dressed in freshly pressed suntans, also without decorations. Neither do they wear neckties. This is Halsey's ship and in the dismal winter of 1942 when he took command of the failing Guadalcanal campaign he banned neckties at his headquarters, the black ties of the navy and the tan of the other services. At that troubled time he wanted nothing to differentiate among the forces fighting the common enemy in his unified command.

Later, at the quarters he occupied at Pearl Harbor when his Third Fleet was between missions, a carved and varnished wooden sign hung in the entrance hall opposite the front

175

door. It greeted visitors with this admonition:

"In your neat black tie, you sure look terrific,

"But you can take it off here, this is still

South Pacific."

Guests were invited to hang their ties of whatever color on an adjacent rack.

Now the American destroyer *Buchanan* pulls alongside. Up the steep stairway hanging along the *Missouri's* starboard side comes General MacArthur, designated Supreme Commander Allied Powers for the occupation. He will conduct this ceremony. Like the rest of the Americans, he is dressed in suntans, wears no decorations and is tieless.

The highest ranking American and foreign officers have lined up now in ranks against the aft bulkhead, 10 to 15 feet behind a rectangular 10-foot-long steel table borrowed from the *Missouri's* wardroom. It is covered with a blue cloth trimmed in white. Two straight chairs stand on opposite sides of the table fore and aft. The rest of the Americans and our Allied guests are lined up along the inboard bulkhead just below us.

Nimitz and Halsey greet the general and his party at the head of the gangway. Then, preceded by the general's Chief of Staff, Lieutenant General Richard K. Sutherland, MacArthur and Nimitz come up the short stairway from the main deck and walk abreast to Halsey's quarters. Contrary to the popular perception, they have been equals throughout the war, supreme commanders in their respective theaters, the Southwest Pacific and the Central Pacific, which later was renamed Pacific Ocean Areas to recognize Nimitz' drive westward. Halsey follows.

Now a small American vessel is sighted moving through the fleet. It comes alongside at 8:50 a.m. Three minutes later, Mamoru Shigemitsu, the Japanese Foreign Minister, struggles to the top of the stairway and onto the main deck at the head of his party. He is hampered by the artificial leg he acquired during a Korean terrorist bombing in Shanghai in 1932 and he limps with a cane.

The ship grows quiet. A grim-faced but very correct American officer conducts them to a cleared area at the forward end of the verandah deck.

There are 11 of them—seven generals and admirals in uniform, three men formally attired in top hats, morning coats and striped pants, and one little guy in a rumpled white suit. They look uncomfortable and unhappy as they assemble in three ranks, Shigemitsu and General Yoshijiro Umetsu in front facing the table and the Allied officers beyond it.

General Hsu Yung-chen of China refuses to look at them. He clears his throat and ostentatiously spits into his handkerchief. The other Chinese glare.

At 8:59 a.m., MacArthur reappears followed by Nimitz, Halsey and Sutherland. MacArthur steps to a small nest of microphones a few feet from the table. It is hooked up to the ship's loudspeaker system and a worldwide radio network.

His face is grim, his voice deep and intense. His hands tremble visibly as he reads a brief statement. He tells the Japanese that he will discharge his responsibilities as Supreme Commander in charge of the occupation of Japan with "justice and tolerance" but will "ensure that the terms of the surrender are fully, properly and faithfully complied with. . . .

"It is my earnest hope, and indeed the hope of all mankind, that from this solemn occasion a better world shall emerge out of the blood and carnage of the past, a world dedicated to the dignity of man and the fulfillmentof his most cherished wish—for freedom, tolerance and justice."

He invites the Japanese to sign the surrender documents, two large bound books, both in English. Shigemitsu limps forward, removing his top hat as he seats himself at the table with some difficulty and begins the distasteful job of signing away his country's sovereignty.

We suspected then that he might soon be convicted as a war criminal but we did not know that he would serve only five years in prison, then rise again to the post of foreign minister, a symbol of the firm but constructive occupation MacArthur was to administer.

He first signs the black-bound copy for the Japanese, then rises to sign the gold-bound Allied copy farther down the table. As he leans over, his cane clatters to the deck. A Japanese aide retrieves it.

Then Umetsu, Chief of the Imperial General Staff steps forward to sign for the Japanese armed forces. It must gall the general, proud leader of the military machine which had swept through Southeast Asia toward what the Japanese thought would be the domination of half the world, to sign a document which says, "We hereby proclaim the unconditional surrender to the Allied Powers of the Japanese General Headquarters and of all armed forces under Japanese control, wherever situated."

Umetsu steps back and MacArthur says, "Will General Wainwright and General Percival step forward while I sign." The two men, an American who had to surrender the Philippines at Corregidor and the Briton who bowed to superior forces at Singapore, take their places behind MacArthur as he seats himself. They are emaciated after nearly four years in Japanese prison camps, their shoulders slightly stooped, but they stand proudly with backbones straight as they come to attention.

Epilogue

Unlike Shigemitsu, MacArthur does not remove his famous cap, the trademark Philippine field marshal's headpiece which he wore throughout the war. It looks as though it's on its last legs, the gilt on the visor tarnished and dull, the top slightly stained.

Signing as Supreme Commander Allied Powers, MacArthur uses five pens. The first he hands to Wainwright, the next to Percival. The next two he lays aside, one to be sent to the National Archives and one to West Point. The fifth is a red fountain pen which he takes from and returns to his breast pocket. It is his wife's.

Returning to the microphones, MacArthur says, "The representative of the United States of America will now sign." Nimitz steps forward, his silvery white hair showing below his cap. His often-friendly blue eyes icy and hard now. He calls for Vice Admiral Forrest C. Sherman, his chief of staff, and Halsey to stand behind him while he signs.

Now MacArthur calls in turn for the representatives of China, the United Kingdom, the USSR, Australia, Canada, France, the Netherlands and New Zealand to sign.

When it is the turn of Admiral Sir Bruce Fraser of the United Kingdom, he uses the two pens MacArthur had laid aside for the Archives and West Point. Then, to the consternation of some of MacArthur's staff, he hands them to an aide who pockets them. An American officer finally retrieved them that afternoon.

Colonel L. Moore Cosgrave of Canada, sixth to sign, places his signature on the line below "Canada" instead of above it. Those who follow also sign on wrong lines. At the end of the ceremony, the Japanese notice this and question it. Sutherland assures them that the document is valid nonetheless, then solves the problem by scratching out the original national designations and rewriting them below the signatures.

As New Zealand signs last for the Allies, the sun breaks through the clouds hiding Mt. Fujiyama. Then MacArthur speaks:

"A way must now be found to preserve the peace because science has given us war of utter destructiveness. We have had our last chance. If we do not devise some greater and more equitable system, Armageddon will be at our door. . ."

His reference, of course, was to the atomic bombs which had wiped out the cities of Hiroshima and Nagasaki on August 6 and 9.

Even though I knew the bombs had killed more than half the populations of the two cities, even though I had read eye-witness accounts of their devastation, it was difficult to comprehend the awful power of those weapons.

Leslie Nakashima, a member of UP's pre-war Tokyo staff, got to Hiroshima on August 22. "There is not a single building standing intact in this city. . ." he wrote. ". . .the railroad station, which was one of the largest in western Japan, no longer exists. The only thing left are its concrete platforms. . . .

"I was dumbfounded at the destruction. . .The center of the city immediately south and west of the station was razed to the ground and there was a sweeping view to the foot of the mountains to the east, south and north. . .what had been a city of 300,000 had vanished. As far as I could see, there were skeletons of only three concrete buildings standing in the city's chief business center."

UP reporter James McGlincy, who had covered the devastating war raids of the war in Europe, visited Hiroshima shortly after the surrender. He called it "undoubtedly the most destroyed city per square mile of all those that have been bombed and shelled in six years of bloody war in

Epilogue

Europe and the Pacific.

"One bomb—that is the key to the most staggering single event of this war. You can ride through Hiroshima and look at it again and again and all the time you say to yourself, 'One bomb did all this.'

". . .In this city, you can see all the ruined cities of the world put together and spread out. In this city, you can see in the eyes of the few Japanese picking through the ruins all of the hate it is possible for a human to muster."

A young Japanese naval lieutenant who was born in Sacramento, California was McGlincy's guide. "How do people feel about us?" McGlincy asked him. "Do they hate us or do they think this is the fortune of war?"

Simply and frankly, the young lieutenant replied, "They hate you."

Some of that I already knew and I learned more later about the horrible potential of nuclear weapons. I've read the criticism that says we could have beaten Japan without dropping the bombs, that the devastation was not necessary. Then I think of the thousands who died on both sides because stubborn Japanese troops refused to give up as they defended Pacific islands far from their homeland, even though their leaders knew the war already was lost.

I'm sure that thousands and thousands more would have died on both sides in the invasion of Japan which already had been planned. The assault on the beaches of the home islands and the battle for the fields and mountains of Kyushu and Honshu would have been no easier than the bloody battles of Guadalcanal, Tarawa, Iwo Jima and Okinawa. The Allied ships would have been closer to the bases of *kamikaze* pilots whose predecessors had been so successful in flying their bomb-laden planes into our ships off Okinawa only a few months earlier.

I think of the thousands who already had died, both in our ranks and theirs, in the horrors of our aerial bombardment of Japan's cities which surely would have continued had Hirohito not surrendered. Nearly ten-million dead, wounded or homeless, the Japanese radio had said a few days earlier. I believe President Truman's decision to drop the bombs was right for these reasons:

1. American POWs were told by their Japanese guards that when the first American landed in Japan, every POW in Japanese hands would be executed—100,000 or more.

2. In late June, President Truman's military advisor, Fleet Admiral William D. Leahy, estimated that 30 to 35% of Americans involved in the invasion of Kyushu would be killed or wounded—230,000 to 270,000.
   Revisionists say such estimates were overstated and it's true that MacArthur earlier had submitted a more optimistic estimate. But, after seeing new intelligence on Japanese plans, MacArthur's chief surgeon revised his estimate of casualties in the Kyushu campaign upward to 395,000. That figure did not include estimates for the later invasion of Honshu.

3. There were reports of Japanese peace feelers in June through the Soviet Union. What Japan proposed then was that the Soviets broker a surrender on Japanese terms after which Japan and the Soviets would team up to dominate Asia. The source of this information is American intercepts of Japanese communications. One of the best-kept secrets of the war and one of our most potent weapons was our ability to crack

their codes.

4. Even after the Hiroshima bomb, Japanese militarists argued vehemently against surrender and it took Emperor Hirohito to make the decision to accept the Allied demand for unconditional surrender.

On March 19, 1996, Dr. Edward Teller, "Father of the Atomic Bomb", in a keynote address at a seminar sponsored by the Admiral Nimitz Museum and Trinity University in San Antonio, Texas, said he had thought for nearly 50 years that explosion of a demonstration bomb 30,000 feet over Tokyo Bay would have been preferable to dropping the bomb on Hiroshima. However, he said that after hearing former POWs in the previous day's discussion describe their mistreatment and the threats against their lives, after hearing from historians who had studied Allied plans for the invasion of Japan, he had changed his mind.

"For the first time," he said, "I had a very real impression of something which almost amounts to a complete moral justification for using the bomb." He said the question was difficult and complicated but "we had to do something to end the war. . .we had to come to the aid of the prisoners of war. . .we had to make peace."

Back on the *Missouri*, MacArthur continues: "Let us pray that peace be now restored to the world and that God will preserve it always. These proceedings are closed."

But they are not quite over.

As MacArthur, Nimitz and Halsey turn toward Halsey's cabin without another glance at the Japanese, the Japanese delegation also turns to depart. In the distance, there is a roar which grows louder and louder.

Out of the south at about a thousand feet comes a formation of nine B-29 Superforts, the big bombers that laid

183

waste to Tokyo and much of Japan, then another and another and more. Following them come scores of other Allied warplanes—Avengers, Hellcats Corsairs, Helldivers and others, nearly a thousand in all. Most of them were not even on the drawing boards on December 7, 1941. They roar up the bay toward Tokyo in a final display of military power over a beaten enemy.

As the Japanese descend the steep gangway along the *Missouri's* side, they carry with them MacArthur's General Order No. 1. It is a detailed and lengthy set of instructions for the surrender of Japanese armed forces throughout Asia, the demilitarization of the nation and the treatment of prisoners of war still in their hands.

It is the beginning of the most remarkable military occupation of a beaten country the world has ever seen, an occupation which, perhaps unintentionally, laid the foundation for a government and an economy which would, within two generations, challenge the victor for world economic supremacy.

In an interview with United Press on September 21, 1945, MacArthur would say that Japan "never again" will become a world power. How wrong he was. He failed to appreciate the potential of the economic and governmental foundation which his own occupation created.

The resurgence of Japan and of West Germany, in what is little more than a tick of the clock of history, is a lesson on the failure of vengeful and cowardly diplomacy and the futility of war.

The seeds of World War II were sown at the end of World War I in the vengeance of the Treaty of Versailles. They were nurtured in the '20s by American isolationism and in the '30s by the uncertain and timid diplomacy that permitted the Japanese invasion of Manchuria in 1931 and the rape of

China, that failed to stop Hitler's first tentative steps of aggression in the Saar and the Rhineland, that refused to intervene when Mussolini invaded Ethiopia.

Consequently, by 1941 Hitler seemed to be on his way to a military victory which would have given Germany control of most of Europe. Japan was pushing its domination of Asia by armed force to the limits of Allied—mostly American—patience.

When the United States in November said, "Stop. No more," the Japanese military executed its secret plan to eliminate the U.S. navy as a threat to expansion.

Less than four years later, Germany and Japan were on their knees, their cities and industrial bases mostly rubble. Less than 40 years after that, their cities and industries had been rebuilt and their economies had reached levels far above those of their pre-war dreams, all without firing a shot.

The roots of their resurgence were in the benign occupation of their lands by the victors; they were watered by billions of dollars of American aid.

In that period, Japan achieved far more as a world economic power than it ever dreamed would be possible through its military dominated pre-war expansion. By the late '80s, Japan had outstripped the United States in many areas of technology. Its automobile industry had Detroit on the run and Americans bewailed the sale of companies, farms and landmark buildings to the former enemy.

In the circumstances of the late '30s and early '40s, World War II was a war which had to be fought, but how wasted were the millions of lives lost or ruined in the six years of that war and the billions of dollars it cost. They were wasted because ruthless and greedy men sought domination by military means instead of through science, industry, education and good will, and because it was a war which

185

diplomatic wisdom and military strength might have averted. Instead, we had vengeance, isolationism and weak-kneed diplomacy. They produced the circumstances which made war inevitable. Have we learned anything from this?

Appendix

President Franklin D. Roosevelt's message to Congress in joint session, December 8, 1941:

Mr. Vice President, Mr. Speaker, members of the Senate and the House of Representatives:

Yesterday, December 7, 1941—a date which will live in infamy—the United States of America was suddenly and deliberately attacked by naval and air forces of the empire of Japan.

The United States was at peace with that nation, and, at the solicitation of Japan, was still in conversation with its government and its Emperor looking toward the maintenance of peace in the Pacific.

Indeed, one hour after Japanese air squadrons had commenced bombing in the American island of Oahu, the Japanese ambassador to the United States and his colleague delivered to our Secretary of State a formal reply to a recent American message. And, while this reply stated that it seemed useless to continue the existing diplomatic negotiations, it contained no threat or hint of war or of armed attack.

It will be recorded that the distance of Hawaii from Japan make it obvious that the attack was deliberately planned many days or even weeks ago. During the intervening time, the Japanese government has deliberately sought to deceive the United States by false statements and expressions of hope for continued peace.

The attack yesterday on the Hawaiian Islands has caused severe damage to American naval and military forces. I regret to tell you that very many American lives have been lost. In addition, American ships have been reported torpedoed on the high seas between San Francisco and Honolulu.

Yesterday, the Japanese government also launched an

attack against Malaya.

Last night Japanese forces attacked Hong Kong.

Last night Japanese forces attacked Guam.

Last night Japanese forces attacked the Philippine Islands.

Last night the Japanese attacked Wake Island.

And this morning the Japanese attacked Midway Island.

Japan has, therefore, undertaken a surprise offensive extending throughout the Pacific area. The facts of yesterday and today speak for themselves. The people of the United States have already formed their opinions and well understand the implications to the very life and safety of our nation.

As Commander in Chief of the Army and Navy, I have directed that all measures be taken for our defense, that always will our whole nation remember the character of the onslaught against us.

No matter how long it may take us to overcome this premeditated invasion, the American people in their righteous might, will win through to absolute victory.

I believe that I interpret the will of Congress and of the people when I assert that we will not only defend ourselves to the uttermost but will make it very certain that this form of treachery shall never again endanger us.

Hostilities exist. There is no blinking at the fact that our people, our territory and our interests are in grave danger.

With confidence in our armed forces, with the unbounding determination of our people, we will gain the inevitable triumph. So help us God.

I ask that the Congress declare that since the unprovoked and dastardly attack by Japan on Sunday, December 7,

1941, a state of war has existed between the United States and the Japanese Empire.

-O-

Text of statement issued by the *White House* December 8, 1941:

American operations against the Japanese attacking force in the neighborhood of the Hawaiian Islands are still continuing. A number of Japanese planes and submarines have been destroyed.

The damage caused to our forces in Oahu in yesterday's attack appears more serious than at first believed.

In Pearl Harbor itself, one old battleship has capsized and several other ships have been seriously damaged.

One destroyer was blown up. Several other small ships were seriously hurt. Army and navy fields were bombed with the resulting destruction of several hangars. A large number of planes were put out of commission.

A number of bombers arrived safely from San Francisco during the engagement—while it was under way. Reinforcement of planes are being rushed and repair work is underway on the ships, planes and ground facilities.

Guam, Wake and Midway Islands and Hong Kong have been attacked. Details of these attacks are lacking.

Two hundred Marines—all that remain in China—have been interned by the Japanese near Tientsin.

The total number of casualties on the island of Oahu are not yet definitely known, but, in all probability, will amount to about 3,000. Nearly half of these are fatalities, the others being wounded. It seems clear from the report that many bombs were dropped in the city of Honolulu, resulting in a small number of casualties.

-O-

Text of the U.S. Navy Department's statement dated

Pearl Harbor

December 5, 1942 on the Japanese attack on Pearl Harbor on December 7, 1941:

On the morning of December 7, 1941, Japanese aircraft temporarily disabled every battleship and most of the aircraft in the Hawaiian area. Other naval vessels, both combatant and auxiliary, were put out of action, and certain shore facilities, especially at the Naval Air Stations, Ford Island and Kaneohe Bay, were damaged. Most of these ships are now back with the Fleet. The aircraft were all replaced within a few days, and interference with facilities was generally limited to a matter of hours.

When the Japanese attacked Pearl Harbor, two surface ship task forces of the Pacific Fleet were carrying out assigned missions at sea, and two such task forces were at their main base following extensive operations at sea. Discounting small craft, 86 ships of the Pacific Fleet were moored at Pearl Harbor. Included in this force were eight battleships, seven cruisers, 28 destroyers and five submarines. No U.S. aircraft carriers were present.

As a result of the Japanese attack, five battleships, the *Arizona, Oklahoma, California, Nevada* and *West Virginia;* three destroyers, the *Shaw, Cassin* and *Downes;* the minelayer *Oglala;* the target ship *Utah,* and a large floating drydock were either sunk or damaged so severely that they would serve no military purposes for some time. In addition, three battleships, the *Pennsylvania, Maryland* and *Tennessee;* three cruisers, the *Helena, Honolulu* and *Raleigh;* the seaplane tender *Curtiss* and the repair ship *Vestal* were damaged.

Of the 19 naval vessels listed above as sunk or damaged, the 26-year old battleship *Arizona* will be the only one permanently and totally lost. Preparations for righting the *Oklahoma* are now in process, although final decision as to the wisdom of accomplishing this work at this time has not been made. The main and auxiliary machinery, approximately 50 percent of the value, of the *Cassin* and *Downes* were saved. The other 15 vessels either have been or will be salvaged and repaired.

Of the eight vessels described in the second sentence of paragraph three, three returned to the Fleet months ago. A number of the vessels described in the first sentence of paragraph three are now in full service, but certain others, which required extensive machinery and intricate electrical overhauling as well as refloating and hull repairing, are not yet ready for battle action. Naval repair yards are taking advantage of these delays to install numerous modernization features and improvement. To designate these vessels by name now would give the enemy information vital to his war plans; similar information regarding enemy ships which our forces have subsequently damaged but not destroyed is denied to us.

On December 15, 1941, only eight days after the Japanese attack and at a time when there was an immediate possibility of the enemy's coming back, the Secretary of the Navy announced that the *Arizona, Shaw, Cassin, Downes, Utah* and *Oglala* had been lost, that the *Oklahoma* had capsized and that other vessels had been damaged. Fortunately, the salvage and repair accomplishments at Pearl Harbor have exceeded the most hopeful expectations.

Eighty naval aircraft of all types were destroyed by the enemy. In addition, the army lost 97 planes on Hickam and Wheeler Fields. Of these, 23 were bombers, 66 were fighters, and eight were other types.

The most serious American losses were in personnel. As a result of the raid on December 7, 1941, 2,117 officers and enlisted men of the Navy and Marine Corps were killed, 960 are still reported as missing and 876 were wounded but survived. The army casualties were as follows: 226 officers and enlisted men were killed or later died of wounds; 396 were wounded, most of whom have now recovered and have returned to duty.

At 7:55 a.m. on December 7, 1941, Japanese dive bombers swarmed over the Army Air Base, Hickam Field, and the Naval Air Station on Ford Island. A few minutes earlier, the Japanese had struck the Naval Air Station at Kaneohe Bay. Bare seconds later, enemy torpedo planes and dive bombers swung in from various sectors to concentrate their attack on the heavy ships at Pearl Harbor. The enemy attack, aided by the element of surprise and based on exact information, was very successful.

Torpedo planes, assisted effectively by dive bombers, constituted the major threat of the first phase of the Japanese attack, lasting approximately a half-hour. Twenty-one torpedo planes made four attacks, and 30 dive bombers came in in eight waves during this period. Fifteen horizontal bombers also participated in this phase of the raid.

Although the Japanese launched their initial attack as a surprise, battleship-ready machine guns opened fire at once and were progressively augmented by the remaining anti-aircraft batteries as all hands promptly were called to general quarters. Machine guns brought down two and damaged others of the first wave of torpedo planes. Practically all battleship anti-aircraft batteries were firing within five minutes; cruisers, within an average time of four minutes, destroyers, opening up machine guns almost immediately, averaged seven minutes in bringing all anti-aircraft guns into action.

From 8:25 to 8:40 a.m., there was a comparative lull in the raid, although air activity continued with sporadic attack by dive and horizontal bombers. This respite was terminated by the appearance of horizontal bombers which crossed and recrossed their targets from various directions and caused serious damage. While the horizontal bombers were continuing their raids, Japanese dive bombers reappeared, probably being the same ones that had participated in earlier attacks; this phase, lasting about a half-hour, was devoted largely to strafing. All enemy aircraft retired by 9:45 a.m.[20]

Prior to the Japanese attack, 202 U.S. naval aircraft of all types on the island of Oahu were in flying condition, but 150 of these were permanently or temporarily disabled by the enemy's concentrated assault, most of them in the first few minutes of the raid. Of the 52 remaining naval aircraft, 38 took to the air on December 7, 1941, the other 14 being ready too late in the day or being blocked from take-off positions. Of necessity, therefore, the Navy was compelled to depend on anti-aircraft fire for its primary defensive weapon, and this condition exposed the fleet to continuous air attack. By coincidence, 18 scout bombing planes from a U.S. aircraft carrier en route arrived at Pearl Harbor during the raid. These are included in the foregoing figures. Four of these scout bombers were shot down, 13 of the remaining 14 taking off again in search of the enemy. Seven patrol planes were in the air when the attack started.

It is difficult to determine the total number of enemy aircraft participating in the raid, but careful analysis of all reports makes it possible to estimate the number as 21 torpedo planes, 48 dive bombers and 36 horizontal bombers, totalling 105 of all types. Undoubtedly certain fighter planes also were present but these are not distinguished by types and are included in the above figures.[21]

The enemy lost 28 aircraft due to navy action. In addition

three submarines of 45 tons each were accounted for.

The damage suffered by the U.S. Pacific Fleet as result of the Japanese attack on December 7, 1941, was most serious, but the repair job now is nearly completed, and thanks to the inspired and unceasing efforts of the naval and civilian personnel attached to the various repair yards, especially at Pearl Harbor itself, this initial handicap soon will be erased forever.

Bibliography
and Work Cited*

1. Prange, Gordon W. *At Dawn We Slept*. 1981. McGraw-Hill Book Company, New York.
2. Halsey, William F. and J. Bryan. *Admiral Halsey's Story*. 1947. McGraw-Hill, New York.
3. Prange, pp 73-77
4. *Ibid* pp 316-319
5. Carroll, J.F. *Oklahoma* crew member, in ship's newspaper of USS *Indianapolis,* December 20, 1941.
6. Tremaine, Frank. United Press dispatch of March24, 1942 from Honolulu, based on U.S. Navy press release of same date, author unknown.
7. Albright, Harry. *Pearl Harbor, Japan's Fatal Blunder*. 1988. Hippocrene Books, Inc. p. 139
8. See appendix for complete text of President Roosevelt's message.
9. Nimitz, Chester W. Hearst newspaper supplement. *The American Weekly.* December 7, 1958.
10. A gunsight from *Ward* is on exhibit in the Pearl Harbor Room of the Nimitz Museum, Fredericksburg, Texas.
11. Prange, pp 495-497
12. *Ibid*, pp 485-495
13. Yarborough, Thomas. Associated Press dispatch in New York *Times.* December 13, 1941.
14. Miyamoto, Kazuo. *Hawaii—End of the Rainbow*. 1964. Bridgeway Press, p. 303.
15. *Ibid*, pp 335-338
16. *Ibid*, pp 340-345
17. UP dispatch of December 20, 1945 from Navy release
18. Miller, S1C Lee in newsletter of USS *Indianapolis* about December 23, 1941. MacArthur, Douglas. Quoted in.
19. UP dispatch from Tokyo September 14, 1941.

20. Historian Gordon W. Prange, who interviewed Japanese planners of the Pearl Harbor attack and commanders and airmen who participated in it, wrote that the Japanese attacked in two waves of 183 and 167 fighters, horizontal bombers, dive bombers and torpedo bombers, launched about 55 minutes apart from six carriers about 220 miles north of Oahu. *At Dawn We Slept,* pp 490-492.
21. Prange wrote that the two waves of attackers totalling 350 planes consisted of 79 fighters, 128 dive bombers, 40 torpedo planes and 103 horizontal bombers.

* Numbers match reference numbers in text.

Chapter Notes

Note: PHA in the following refers to hearings before the Joint Committee on the Investigation of the Pearl Harbor Attack (Congress). The PHA material I've used was found in Prange's *At Dawn We Slept*, but I have not always cited Prange since PHA material is in the public domain. Also, much of it was widely reported at the time and since.

Chapter 1: Kimmel and Short December 6 activities from Prange pp. 481-482 citing PHA. Activities of others from Brown and Albright letters and personal knowledge.

Chapter 6: From Willet's letter and phone conversation.

Chapter 7: Largely from Pearl Harbor anniversary (20th?) story written by Howard Case for UP.

Chapter 8: From newspaper clip (UP) in scrapbook and phone conversation with Sam Brown.

Chapter 9: From Brown's letter. Letter did not identify by name the commander who was acting C.O. I told Sam in phone conversation that normally I'd want the name but, in this case, I thought it better not to name the man. He might very well have served with distinction after that day. Sam agreed and I inferred from what Sam said that he was a good officer.

Chapter 10: Most of this chapter from Jim Gray letter and phone conversation and *Fighting Six* diary. Location of *Saratoga*, most ship movements and Nichol quote from Prange, citing PHA.

Chapter 11: Most of this chapter from memory, diary, clips in scrapbook. Hull, Nomura, Kurusu meeting from New York *Times* December 8, 1941.

Chapter 12: This chapter from memory and scrapbook clips.

Chapter 14: Raid on Japanese consulate from *Star Bulletin* clips in scrapbook and Prange p. 562 citing PHA and Van Kuren (Honolulu police officer) report. Anne Brown- Janet Hahn incident from Anne's letter.

Chapter 15: Material on Yoshikawa is from Prange as noted. Much of Prange's material, which is much more extensive than anything I've used, came from Prange interview with Yoshikawa. Material on Kurusu airport interview is from copies of my cables and memory.

Chapter 16: Carroll material from eye-witnesses. He wrote for USS *Indianapolis* ship's newspaper which I picked up during cruise aboard her in January, 1942. Remainder from clip of my UP story written from navy press release weeks after Pearl Harbor attack.

Chapter 17: From Sam's letter and phone conversation.

Chapter 19: Most reports in this chapter are from scrapbook clips, a few from New York *Times*.

Chapter 20: Newspaper reports from clips and tearsheets in scrapbook. Albright story as cited. Other material from diary and memory.

Chapter 21: From diary, memory and Anne Brown's letter.

Chapter 22. FDR speech and related material from New York *Times* December 9, 1941, Knox press release and related from New York *Times* December 17, 1941, navy communiqué from navy text.

Chapter 23: Statistics on Oahu's defenses from Albright. Nimitz quotes are from an article he wrote for the Hearst newspaper supplement, *The American Weekly* of December 7, 1958 as quoted in Albright's book. *Yorktown* repair in Albright p. 338.

Chapter 24: Most material in this chapter is from scrapbook clips. Information on army activities also from Albright book. Most of *Ward* action from Prange, p. 596, citing Outerbridge and naval material. Washington portion of delayed message from Marshall to Short per Prange pp. 494-495 citing PHA. Material regarding radar sighting from memory, Albright book, Prange. Taylor, Welch, Rasmussen material from clips, citations, Prange. Yarborough story from his AP story in New York *Times* about December 12, 1941.

Chapter 25: From Gray's letter, phone and Fighting Six diary.

Chapter 26: Story of rumor in 2nd paragraph is from diary of William McCain, a gunnery officer on USS *Indianapolis* in 1941-42, as published in Savannah *Morning News* December 7, 1989 from Cox News Service. I never actually talked to McCain, as far as I can remember, but he is still listed as an ensign on the *Indianapolis'* roster dated January 1, 1942 which I obtained when I was aboard her. The ship was full of rumors at the time and this was one of them, although I did not note it then in my own diary. Material about detention of Japanese is from Miyamoto's book as cited. Exploits of 100th Battalion and 442nd Regimental Combat Team are matter of public record.

Chapter 29: Material on *Nevada* action is from eye-witnesses by former crew members printed in USS *Indianapolis* ship's newspaper while I was aboard, from clip of UP story from navy press releases quoting unidentified officers which, when compared with material in Prange, made it evident that Ruff was one of those quoted by Navy release, and from Prange pp. 515, 535-536 citing interviews in *Nevada's* log.

Index

About the Authors

Kay (Katherine) Tremaine's telephone dispatch to the United Press in San Francisco from Honolulu on December 7, 1941 was the first eye-witness account of the Japanese attack on Pearl Harbor to reach the mainland. Her husband Frank became an instant war correspondent that Sunday morning by looking out of his front windows. What he saw was a plume of black smoke from the bombed ships. As UP's Honolulu bureau manager his FLASH—the highest category of breaking new story—alerted the wire service that all was not well in paradise.

Determined to remain in Hawaii with her husband after the Pacific War began, Kay got a job with the Army Signal Corps as a cryptographer, then as a reporter with Honolulu's major newspapers the *Star-Bulletin* and then the rival *Advertiser*. Later, on the mainland, she turned to school teaching, primarily foreign languages and English.

The Tremaine's love story of more than 50 years began in the 6th grade in Pasadena, California. A later career in the United Press led Frank to assignments in Tokyo, Korea, during most of that conflict, Mexico City and Los Angeles, ending with his retirement as senior vice-president of United Press International in New York in 1981.

Kay notes wryly that Frank managed to be in the South Pacific when daughter Nancy was born in Honolulu and in Mexico City when son Pancho arrived in Pasadena, California. "Frank has never been home for the birth of a baby, a 2-o'clock feeding, or a major move." He was present for their final move, however. Kay wished he'd been on a trip!

Arriving Honolulu aboard SS Matsonia
for our new assignment, June 1940

Today